I0446259

Strategies, Insights, and Innovations

MEDIA RELATIONS

Mastering the Art of Engaging with the Media

OSMAN KARAKAS

About Book

Book Title: Media Relations:

Strategies, Insights, and Innovations

Subtitle: *Mastering the Art of Engaging with the Media*

Format: Word/PDF

Size: 6X9 inches - 15.24X22.89 cm

Total Pages: 158

E-mail: okarakas@hotmail.com

Web: www.osmankarakas.com

CONTENTS

Preface:

In the bustling corridors of today's interconnected world, where information travels at the speed of light and perceptions shape realities, the role of media relations stands as a lighthouse guiding organizations through the seas of public discourse. As we delve into the pages of this handbook, we embark on a journey that explores the intricacies, strategies, and innovations defining contemporary media relations.

Media Relations: Strategies, Insights, and Innovations is not just a book; it's a compendium of wisdom gathered from the trenches of real-world interactions, the boardrooms of successful campaigns, and the minds of thought leaders shaping the future of public relations. In these pages, we navigate the nuances of building meaningful relationships with journalists, crafting compelling narratives, and harnessing the power of digital media to amplify our messages.

The digital age has ushered in unprecedented opportunities and challenges, transforming the very fabric of media relations. With the rise of social media, influencers, and real-time news cycles, the landscape in which we operate has become both dynamic and complex. However, it is precisely in this complexity that the art and science of media relations find their canvas.

As media professionals, our ability to adapt, innovate, and resonate with our audience defines our success.

This handbook is designed as a compass, offering guidance to both seasoned media relations veterans and those just beginning their journey. Through meticulously crafted chapters, we explore the fundamentals of media relations, from understanding the core principles to dissecting case studies that illuminate successful strategies. We delve into the ethical considerations that underpin our interactions, unravel the secrets of crisis communication, and peer into the future, where artificial intelligence and immersive technologies shape the narratives of tomorrow.

Each chapter is a testament to the collaboration of experts, the dedication of professionals, and the curiosity of learners. It is an amalgamation of experiences, research, and insights that have been carefully woven together to provide a holistic understanding of media relations in the modern age.

As you embark on this exploration, we encourage you to approach these pages with an open mind and a thirst for knowledge. Media relations is not a one-size-fits-all endeavor; it is a dynamic, ever-evolving practice that demands creativity, empathy, and strategic acumen. Whether you are a communications professional steering a multinational corporation through the currents of public perception or a budding PR enthusiast eager to make your mark, the insights within these pages are tailored to enrich your journey.

On this odyssey through the realms of media relations, may you find inspiration, practical wisdom, and the confidence to navigate the multifaceted challenges of our profession. Here's to mastering the art of engaging with the media, forging meaningful connections, and shaping narratives that resonate in the hearts and minds of our audiences.

Welcome to a world where stories unfold, perceptions transform, and media relations becomes not just a practice, but a craft.

Warm regards,

Osman Karakas

Author

Chapter 1: Introduction to Media Relations

Overview of Media Relations
Media relations is the strategic communication process that organizations utilize to establish and maintain relationships with journalists, bloggers, influencers, and other key figures in the media industry. In an age where information spreads rapidly, mastering the art of media relations is essential for businesses, non-profits, and individuals alike. This chapter serves as a foundational exploration of the field, delving into its significance and evolution.

Definition and Importance

Media relations involves managing the relationship between an organization and the media to ensure accurate and favorable coverage. It's not just about issuing press releases; it's about building trust, credibility, and understanding between the organization and the media outlets. Understanding the power of media relations is crucial for shaping public perception and managing reputation.

Media relations encompass a multifaceted approach to communication that involves managing the relationship between an organization and the media landscape. It goes far beyond the mere distribution of press releases; it is an ongoing process rooted in building robust connections, trust, and mutual understanding between an organization and various media outlets. This section delves into the core aspects of the definition and sheds light on its pivotal importance in the realm of public relations.

Managing Relationships for Accurate and Favorable Coverage

At its essence, media relations is about fostering a symbiotic relationship. Organizations seek to provide journalists with accurate, timely, and relevant information, while journalists rely on these organizations as credible sources for news stories. This reciprocity is fundamental in shaping public perception. By cultivating a positive relationship with the media, organizations can influence how their stories are presented, ensuring accurate and favorable coverage.

Beyond Press Releases: Building Trust and Credibility

While press releases are an essential tool, effective media relations extend far beyond these formal communications. It involves cultivating personal connections with journalists, understanding their interests, and tailoring pitches to align with their beats. Trust and credibility are the cornerstones of successful media relations. When journalists trust an organization to provide accurate and valuable information, they are more likely to cover its news and events in a positive light. Establishing this trust takes time, consistency, and a keen understanding of the media landscape.

Shaping Public Perception and Managing Reputation

In the digital age, where information spreads rapidly through various channels, managing public perception is paramount. Media relations plays a pivotal role in shaping how an organization is perceived by its target audience. Positive media coverage enhances credibility, instills confidence among stakeholders, and can even influence customer behavior. Conversely, mishandled media relations can lead to reputational damage, which can be challenging to recover from. By mastering the art of media relations, organizations can proactively manage their reputation, respond effectively to crises, and maintain a favorable image in the eyes of the public.

In summary, media relations is the linchpin of effective communication between organizations and the media. It is a strategic endeavor focused on building enduring relationships, ensuring accurate and favorable coverage, and safeguarding the organization's reputation. Understanding its nuances is essential for anyone involved in the fields of public relations, marketing, or corporate communications.

Evolution of Media Relations in the Digital Age

With the advent of digital technology, media relations has undergone a transformative shift. Social media platforms, online news portals, podcasts, and live streaming have revolutionized how information is disseminated. Organizations now have a plethora of channels to engage with their audience directly. This section explores how media relations has adapted to these changes, emphasizing the importance of a digital presence and online reputation management.

The digital age has ushered in a transformative era for media relations, fundamentally altering how organizations interact with the media and the public. The rise of digital technology, including social media platforms, online news portals, podcasts, and live streaming, has revolutionized the dissemination of information. This evolution has reshaped the strategies and tactics employed in media relations, emphasizing the need for a strong digital presence and adept online reputation management.

Rise of Social Media Platforms

Social media platforms such as Facebook, Twitter, Instagram, LinkedIn, and TikTok have become integral to media relations strategies. These platforms provide a direct channel for organizations to engage with their audience in real-time. Through social media, organizations can share news, updates, and multimedia content instantly, fostering a sense of community and interactivity. Moreover, social media platforms allow for direct communication with journalists, bloggers, and influencers, enabling more personalized and targeted outreach.

Online News Portals and Digital Journalism

The proliferation of online news portals and digital journalism has transformed the way news is consumed. Traditional print media has transitioned into the digital realm, enabling instant access to news stories from around the world. For media relations professionals, this shift necessitates adapting strategies to cater to online audiences. Crafting digital-friendly press releases, optimizing content for search engines (SEO), and understanding the dynamics of online journalism have become crucial skills. Moreover, online news portals often allow for multimedia content integration, enabling organizations to convey their messages through a combination of text, images, and videos.

Podcasts and Live Streaming

Podcasts and live streaming have emerged as powerful mediums for storytelling and brand promotion. Podcasts offer a platform for in-depth discussions, interviews, and thought leadership content, reaching audiences during their commute, workouts, or leisure time. Live streaming, facilitated by platforms like YouTube, Facebook Live, and Instagram Live, enables real-time interaction with a global audience. Organizations can host live Q&A sessions, product launches, behind-the-scenes tours, and events, fostering direct engagement and authenticity.

Importance of Digital Presence

In the digital age, having a robust online presence is non-negotiable. A well-designed website serves as the central hub of information, providing comprehensive details about the organization, its mission, products, and services. Social media profiles reinforce this presence, offering dynamic, interactive platforms to engage with diverse audiences. A cohesive digital presence not only enhances visibility but also instills confidence among stakeholders, including journalists, investors, customers, and the general public.

Online Reputation Management

With the vast digital landscape comes the challenge of managing online reputation effectively. Online reviews, comments on social media, and news articles can significantly impact public perception. Media relations professionals must actively monitor online conversations, respond to comments and reviews professionally, and address misinformation promptly. Proactive reputation management involves cultivating positive online interactions, showcasing transparency, and demonstrating a commitment to addressing concerns. Tools and techniques, such as sentiment analysis and online monitoring software, aid in gauging public sentiment and shaping responses accordingly.

In essence, the evolution of media relations in the digital age necessitates a strategic blend of traditional PR tactics and innovative digital approaches. Embracing the diverse array of digital platforms, understanding the nuances of online communication, and mastering the art of online reputation management are integral to thriving in today's media landscape.

Feel free to let me know if you would like to explore specific digital platforms in more detail or if there are other aspects of media relations you'd like to delve into further!

Expanding Future Trends in Media Relations

The future of media relations is intricately tied to technological advancements and changing audience behaviors. Artificial intelligence, big data analytics, and machine learning are reshaping how organizations interact with the media. Moreover, understanding the dynamics of social media algorithms and leveraging virtual and augmented reality for immersive storytelling are becoming integral parts of media relations strategies. This chapter provides a sneak peek into these emerging trends, preparing readers for the evolving landscape of media relations.

The landscape of media relations is constantly evolving, driven by technological advancements and shifts in audience behaviors. To stay ahead in this dynamic environment, media relations professionals must adapt to emerging trends that are reshaping the way organizations interact with the media and the public. This section explores these future trends, offering insights into the transformative technologies and strategies that are redefining the field of media relations.

Artificial Intelligence (AI) and Machine Learning

Artificial intelligence and machine learning algorithms are revolutionizing media relations by enabling data-driven insights and automation. AI-powered tools analyze vast amounts of data, including media coverage, social media mentions, and audience sentiments. These analyses provide invaluable insights into media trends, enabling organizations to refine their strategies and tailor their pitches to specific journalists or outlets. Moreover, AI-driven chatbots and virtual assistants are being used to handle routine media inquiries, freeing up human resources for more strategic tasks. Machine learning algorithms can also predict media trends, helping organizations proactively shape their narratives and stay ahead of the curve.

Big Data Analytics

The proliferation of data from various sources, including social media, online news platforms, and customer interactions, has given rise to big data analytics in media relations. Analyzing big data helps organizations identify patterns, preferences, and emerging topics among their target audience. Media professionals can leverage these insights to craft compelling narratives that resonate with their audience. Understanding the data-driven preferences of journalists and media consumers allows for more precise and effective media outreach, ensuring that pitches align with the interests of both journalists and their readers.

Social Media Algorithms and Engagement Strategies

Social media platforms continually update their algorithms, affecting how content is displayed and shared. Media relations professionals must stay abreast of these changes to optimize their social media strategies. Understanding the nuances of social media algorithms enables organizations to amplify their reach and engagement. Crafting content that aligns with these algorithms, whether through interactive posts, videos, or live streaming, enhances visibility and encourages audience interaction. Moreover, social listening tools analyze social media conversations, helping organizations gauge public sentiment and adapt their media strategies accordingly.

Virtual and Augmented Reality (VR/AR) for Immersive Storytelling

Virtual and augmented reality technologies are transforming media relations by offering immersive storytelling experiences. VR and AR applications allow organizations to create virtual press conferences, product demonstrations, and interactive experiences. Journalists and audiences can engage with content in a three-dimensional space, enhancing their understanding and emotional connection with the brand. Immersive storytelling not only captures attention but also creates memorable experiences, making it an impactful tool for media outreach. Media professionals are exploring VR/AR applications in press releases, media events, and product launches, providing journalists with a unique perspective and enhancing media coverage.

Preparing for the Evolving Landscape

As media relations enters this era of technological innovation, it is crucial for professionals to adapt and embrace these trends. Staying informed about AI applications, big data analytics, social media algorithms, and immersive technologies equips media relations practitioners with the tools to navigate the evolving landscape effectively. By integrating these technologies into their strategies, organizations can forge stronger connections with the media, craft compelling narratives, and engage audiences in novel and impactful ways.

In summary, the future of media relations is shaped by the synergy of technology and audience behavior. Embracing AI, big data analytics, understanding social media algorithms, and leveraging VR/AR for immersive storytelling are key strategies for staying relevant and impactful in the ever-changing world of media relations.

Chapter 2: Establishing Strong Media Relations

Locally, Nationally, and Internationally

Building and nurturing relationships with the media, whether at the local, national, or international level, is a nuanced process that demands careful planning, strategic outreach, and genuine engagement. Media relations professionals play a vital role in creating and maintaining these connections, not only for companies but also for government authorities, political figures, NGOs, and international organizations. This chapter outlines effective strategies, common mistakes to avoid, and practical tips for establishing successful media relations across various sectors.

2.1. Research and Targeting:

- **Identify Key Media Outlets:** Research local, national, and international media outlets relevant to your sector. Understand their focus, audience, and editorial guidelines.

One of the foundational steps in establishing successful media relations is identifying the right media outlets to target. Whether you are working on a local, national, or international scale, conducting thorough research is essential. Here's how you can effectively identify key media outlets in your sector:

Understanding the Local Landscape:

1. **Local Media Directories:** Utilize local media directories or databases specific to your region. These resources often categorize media outlets based on their focus areas, making it easier to identify relevant ones.

2. **Community Newspapers and Magazines:** Don't overlook community-based media. Local newspapers, magazines, and online platforms cater to specific communities and can provide valuable exposure.

3. **Industry Associations:** Check industry-specific associations and organizations. They often have partnerships with media outlets catering to the sector.

National and International Research:

1. **Industry Reports:** Industry reports often mention media outlets that cover specific sectors extensively. Research industry reports and market analyses to identify prominent media players.

2. **Media Monitoring Tools:** Invest in media monitoring tools that allow you to track media outlets, their coverage, and their influence. These tools provide insights into the outlets that are actively engaged in your industry.

3. **Social Media Platforms:** Follow media outlets on social media platforms. Social media profiles provide real-time updates on their focus areas and the stories they are covering.

Understanding Their Focus, Audience, and Editorial Guidelines:

1. **Review Previous Coverage:** Study the outlets' previous coverage related to your sector. Understand the angles they take, the type of stories they prioritize, and the tone of their reporting.

2. **Identify Targeted Audience:** Determine the audience demographics of each outlet. Consider factors such as age, gender, profession, and interests. Align your messaging with the outlet's audience profile.

3. **Editorial Guidelines:** Familiarize yourself with the editorial guidelines of the outlets you are targeting. Adhering to their guidelines increases the likelihood of your content being considered for publication.

Building a Media Database:

1. **Create a Comprehensive Database:** Develop a detailed database that includes contact information for journalists, editors, and producers. Categorize them based on their specific areas of interest.

2. **Regularly Update the Database:** Media landscapes are constantly evolving. Regularly update your database to include new contacts and remove outdated ones to maintain accuracy.

Utilizing Public Relations Agencies and Consultants:

1. **PR Agencies:** If feasible, consider hiring a reputable PR agency with expertise in your sector. They often have

extensive media networks and can facilitate introductions.

2. **Consult with Media Relations Experts:** Seek advice from experienced media relations professionals. Their insights can be invaluable in identifying the most relevant outlets and approaching them effectively.

By diligently researching and targeting media outlets, you lay the groundwork for effective media outreach. Understanding the media landscape, their audience, and their editorial preferences enables you to craft pitches and press releases tailored to each outlet, increasing the likelihood of favorable coverage.

Feel free to let me know if you would like to explore other sections within this chapter or if you have specific questions related to media relations!

2.2. Segment Your Audience:

Categorize media outlets based on their coverage areas. Tailor your pitches and press releases according to their specific interests.

Segmenting your media audience is a strategic approach that allows you to target specific outlets more effectively. By categorizing media outlets based on their coverage areas, you can tailor your communication to align with their interests and increase the relevance of your pitches and press releases. Here's how you can do it:

Understanding Media Segmentation:

1. **Identify Coverage Areas:** Analyze the previous content of each media outlet. Determine the topics, industries, or themes they predominantly cover. This analysis helps you identify their specific coverage areas.

2. **Categorize Outlets:** Group media outlets into categories based on their focus. For example, categorize outlets into sectors such as technology, healthcare, finance, lifestyle, or regional news. Each category represents a segment of your media audience.

Tailoring Your Communication:

1. **Craft Targeted Pitches:** Once you've segmented the outlets, craft pitches that are tailored to each category. Customize your pitches to highlight aspects of your story that are most relevant to the specific sector the outlet covers. For instance, emphasize the technological innovations for tech-focused outlets and community impact for regional news.

2. **Personalize Press Releases:** Similarly, customize your press releases for different segments. Modify the language, tone, and examples to resonate with the interests of the particular sector. Personalization enhances the chances of your content being deemed newsworthy by the journalists.

Benefits of Audience Segmentation:

1. **Increased Relevance:** Segmentation ensures that your pitches are highly relevant to the media outlets you approach. Journalists are more likely to engage with content that aligns with their area of expertise and interest.

2. **Higher Response Rates:** Targeted communication increases the likelihood of positive responses. Journalists are more receptive to pitches that demonstrate a clear understanding of their beat and interests.

3. **Enhanced Relationships:** Tailoring your communication demonstrates your respect for the journalists' time and expertise. It fosters a positive impression and lays the foundation for a more fruitful and enduring relationship.

Best Practices for Audience Segmentation:

1. **Regularly Update Segments:** Media landscapes evolve. Regularly update your segments to reflect changes in the focus areas of media outlets. Stay informed about shifts in editorial priorities.

2. **Research Journalists:** Within each outlet, research specific journalists who cover relevant topics. Tailor your pitches not just based on the outlet's segment but also considering the individual journalist's preferences and past work.

3. **Track Responses:** Keep track of responses to your pitches based on the segments. Analyze which segments are more responsive and refine your strategies accordingly.

In summary, audience segmentation is a pivotal step in media relations. It ensures that your communication efforts are precise, relevant, and engaging. By understanding the coverage areas of media outlets and tailoring your pitches and press releases accordingly, you significantly enhance your chances of securing meaningful media coverage and building lasting relationships with journalists.

2.3. Create Media Databases:

Maintain up-to-date databases with contact information of journalists, editors, and producers. Use specialized media databases to expand your network.

Building and Maintaining Valuable Contacts

Creating and maintaining a robust media database is fundamental to successful media relations. It forms the backbone of your outreach efforts, enabling you to establish meaningful connections with journalists, editors, and producers. Here's how to create and leverage effective media databases:

Building a Comprehensive Database:

1. **Identify Contacts:** Begin by identifying journalists, editors, and producers relevant to your industry or sector. This includes professionals from local, national, and international outlets. Research their bylines, recent articles, and contributions to understand their expertise.

2. **Gather Contact Information:** Collect accurate contact details, including email addresses, phone numbers, and social media profiles. Ensure the information is up-to-date and regularly verify the contacts to maintain accuracy.

3. **Categorize Contacts:** Categorize your contacts based on their roles, areas of coverage, and the outlets they represent. This categorization helps in targeted outreach, ensuring your pitches reach the right individuals.

Utilizing Specialized Media Databases:

1. **Explore Media Database Services:** Consider using specialized media database services. These platforms offer comprehensive databases of journalists across various beats and outlets. Subscribing to these services can provide access to a wider network and save time on manual research.

2. **Stay Updated:** Media databases are dynamic. Journalists change roles, outlets, or beats. Stay updated with these changes to ensure your pitches reach the right contacts. Regularly update your database with

new additions and remove outdated or irrelevant contacts.

Expanding Your Network:

1. **Attend Industry Events:** Participate in industry events, conferences, and networking sessions. These gatherings provide opportunities to meet journalists in person, exchange contact information, and establish initial connections.

2. **Follow Social Media:** Follow journalists and media outlets on social media platforms. Social media profiles often provide insights into their current projects and interests. Engage with their content professionally to initiate conversations.

Benefits of a Well-Maintained Database:

1. **Efficient Outreach:** A curated media database streamlines your outreach efforts. Instead of sending generic pitches, you can craft personalized messages tailored to each recipient, increasing the likelihood of positive responses.

2. **Increased Response Rates:** Journalists appreciate targeted and relevant pitches. When your communication aligns with their interests, they are more likely to engage with your content, leading to higher response rates.

3. **Building Relationships:** Maintaining an updated media database enables you to nurture relationships

over time. By understanding journalists' preferences and keeping them informed about your industry developments, you foster enduring connections.

Best Practices for Database Management:

1. **Regular Updates:** Schedule regular updates for your media database. Even minor changes in contact details or beats can impact the success of your outreach efforts.

2. **Personalization:** When reaching out to journalists, reference their recent work or interests. Personalization demonstrates your familiarity with their expertise and enhances your credibility.

3. **Data Security:** Ensure data security and compliance with relevant regulations when storing and managing journalists' contact information.

   In summary, creating and maintaining a well-organized media database is indispensable in media relations. Whether through manual research or specialized media database services, investing in a comprehensive database pays off in the form of efficient outreach, increased responses, and the cultivation of enduring professional relationships with members of the media.

2.4 Building Genuine Relationships in Media Relations

Building genuine relationships with journalists and media professionals is a cornerstone of successful media relations. These relationships are built on trust, mutual respect, and a clear understanding of each other's needs. Here are key strategies for building authentic connections with the media:

Personalized Outreach:

1. **Research and Customization:** Before reaching out, research the journalist's work thoroughly. Understand their beat, writing style, and recent articles. Craft personalized pitches that directly relate to their interests and expertise. Referencing their past work in your pitch demonstrates that you value their perspective.

2. **Addressing Journalists by Name:** Address journalists by their names in your communications. This small gesture adds a personal touch, showing that your message is intended specifically for them and not part of a mass distribution.

3. **Timely and Relevant Pitches:** Time your pitches appropriately, aligning them with current events or trends in the journalist's beat. A well-timed pitch that is relevant to their ongoing coverage is more likely to capture their attention.

Face-to-Face Meetings:

1. **Arrange One-on-One Meetings:** Whenever possible, arrange face-to-face meetings with journalists and media professionals. These meetings provide a platform

for in-depth discussions, allowing you to explain your story or organization thoroughly.

2. **Informal Settings:** Consider meeting journalists in informal settings like coffee shops or casual events. Such settings can foster more relaxed and open conversations, allowing for a genuine connection to develop.

3. **Active Listening:** During meetings, practice active listening. Understand the journalist's needs, concerns, and interests. Tailor your discussions to address their questions and provide valuable insights.

Attending Media Events:

1. **Participate Actively:** Attend press conferences, media briefings, and industry events related to your sector. Actively participate in discussions and engage with journalists. Be prepared to share your expertise and insights on relevant topics.

2. **Networking Opportunities:** Use these events as networking opportunities. Approach journalists and introduce yourself. Exchange business cards and express genuine interest in their work. Networking establishes your presence and helps you be remembered in the future.

3. **Follow-Up:** After media events, follow up with journalists you met. Send a brief email expressing your pleasure at having met them and reiterating your willingness to provide further information or assistance.

Personalize each follow-up email to remind them of your conversation.

Building Lasting Relationships:

1. **Consistent Communication:** Maintain consistent but not overwhelming communication with journalists. Keep them updated about your organization's developments, but avoid spamming their inboxes. Provide valuable insights and expert opinions even outside of specific pitches.

2. **Be a Resource:** Position yourself as a reliable resource. Be available for comments, interviews, and background information. Journalists appreciate experts who are accessible and responsive.

3. **Show Gratitude:** Express gratitude when journalists cover your stories. A simple thank-you email or note demonstrates your appreciation for their work and fosters a positive relationship.

In summary, building genuine relationships in media relations involves personalized and respectful communication, face-to-face interactions, and active participation in media events. These efforts not only enhance your chances of securing positive media coverage but also establish a foundation for long-term, mutually beneficial relationships with journalists and media professionals. Remember, sincerity and authenticity are key in nurturing these connections.

2.5. Effective Communication in Media Relations

Effective communication is at the heart of successful media relations. It involves not only the content of your message but also the timing and manner in which it is delivered. Here are the key components of effective communication in media relations:

Clear and Concise Messages:

1. **Clarity is Key:** Craft messages that are clear, concise, and to the point. Avoid jargon and technical language that might confuse your audience. Journalists appreciate straightforward information that can be easily understood by their readers or viewers.

2. **Newsworthiness:** Focus on newsworthy angles in your messages. Highlight the aspects of your story that are unique, timely, or have a significant impact. A compelling angle increases the likelihood of your story being picked up by journalists.

3. **Tailor the Message:** Customize your message for different media outlets and journalists. While the core information remains the same, tailor your language and emphasis to align with the specific interests of each outlet or individual. Personalization enhances relevance and engagement.

Timely Responses:

1. **Quick Turnaround:** Respond promptly to media inquiries, whether they come via email, phone, or social

media. Journalists often work on tight deadlines, and a swift response demonstrates your professionalism and cooperation.

2. **Acknowledge Receipt:** Even if you need time to gather detailed information, acknowledge receipt of the inquiry promptly. Let the journalist know that you are working on their request, which provides them with reassurance that their query is being addressed.

3. **Set Expectations:** If you cannot provide a complete response immediately, communicate a realistic timeline. Inform the journalist when they can expect to receive the information they require. Transparency fosters understanding and trust.

Media Training:

1. **Preparation is Key:** Provide media training to your spokespersons, whether they are company executives, experts, or public relations representatives. Training equips them with the skills and confidence needed for interviews, ensuring they can effectively convey your organization's message.

2. **Message Consistency:** Media training helps ensure that your spokespersons deliver consistent messages across different interviews and media platforms. Consistency reinforces your key points and strengthens your brand image.

3. **Handling Difficult Questions:** Training prepares spokespersons to handle challenging or sensitive

questions effectively. Techniques such as bridging, redirecting, and providing context enable them to navigate difficult situations while staying on message.

In summary, effective communication in media relations involves delivering clear, concise, and newsworthy messages tailored to specific audiences. Timely responses to media inquiries demonstrate professionalism and enhance your credibility. Additionally, media training equips your spokespersons with the skills needed to handle interviews confidently and consistently. By focusing on these aspects, you not only increase your chances of positive media coverage but also strengthen your organization's reputation and relationships with journalists.

2.6. Common Mistakes to Avoid in Media Relations

Navigating the media landscape requires finesse, and avoiding common pitfalls is essential for building and maintaining positive relationships with journalists. Here are key mistakes to steer clear of in your media relations efforts:

1. Generic Pitches:

Mistake: Sending generic, one-size-fits-all pitches to multiple media outlets without customization.

Solution: Tailor each pitch to the specific outlet and journalist. Personalization demonstrates that you've done your homework and value their unique perspective. Reference their past work or recent articles to show that your pitch aligns with their interests and expertise.

Impact: Generic pitches are often ignored, as journalists can easily identify them. Personalized pitches, on the other hand, capture attention and increase the likelihood of positive responses.

2. Ignoring Journalists' Preferences:

Mistake: Disregarding journalists' communication preferences and follow-up methods.

Solution: Respect journalists' preferences, whether they prefer email, phone calls, or social media. Pay attention to their preferred mode of communication and adapt your approach accordingly. Additionally, be mindful of their preferred time for follow-ups.

Impact: Ignoring journalists' preferences can lead to frustration and a negative perception of your organization. Adhering to their preferred communication methods enhances your professionalism and fosters a positive working relationship.

3. Overpromising and Underdelivering:

Mistake: Making promises or commitments that your organization cannot fulfill.

Solution: Be honest and transparent about what you can offer. Avoid overhyping your story or making exaggerated claims. Deliver on what you promise, and if challenges arise, communicate proactively and professionally.

Impact: Overpromising and underdelivering damages your credibility and reputation. Journalists rely on accurate information; if they feel misled, they may avoid working with you in the future.

Additional Tips to Avoid Mistakes:

1. **Thorough Research:** Research the media outlet, journalist, and their previous work before reaching out. Understanding their style and preferences helps you tailor your communication effectively.

2. **Build Relationships:** Focus on building relationships rather than seeking immediate coverage. Long-lasting relationships yield more meaningful and sustained media attention.

3. **Professionalism:** Maintain a high level of professionalism in all interactions. Be courteous, respectful, and responsive. Even if a pitch is declined, respond graciously and express gratitude for the consideration.

4. **Feedback Loop:** Encourage journalists to provide feedback on your interactions. Understanding their perspective can improve future engagements.

5. **Learn from Rejections:** Rejections are part of the process. Use them as learning opportunities. If a pitch

is declined, politely ask for feedback to understand how you can improve your approach.

In summary, avoiding common mistakes in media relations requires a combination of research, professionalism, transparency, and adaptability. By tailoring your pitches, respecting journalists' preferences, and being honest about what you can offer, you can foster positive relationships and enhance your organization's media coverage. Remember, every interaction is an opportunity to strengthen your reputation in the media industry.

2.7. Tips and Recommendations for Successful Media Relations

Navigating the world of media relations is not just about securing coverage; it's about fostering enduring relationships built on trust, reliability, and mutual respect. Here are key tips and recommendations to enhance your media relations strategies:

1. Cultivate Trust:

Tip: Be Transparent and Honest: Transparency is the foundation of trust in media relations. Be open about your organization's goals, achievements, and challenges. Honesty, even in difficult situations, enhances your credibility.

Tip: Reliability Matters: Consistently deliver accurate and reliable information. Journalists rely on trustworthy sources; being reliable ensures that journalists turn to you for credible insights and stories.

Impact: Building trust with journalists establishes you as a go-to source. Trustworthy relationships lead to more favorable coverage and increased credibility for your organization.

2. Focus on Long-Term Relationships:

Tip: Nurture Relationships: Instead of chasing immediate coverage, invest in building enduring relationships. Regularly engage with journalists even when you don't have a story to pitch. This consistent presence keeps your organization on their radar.

Tip: Understand Their Needs: Take the time to understand what journalists need and how you can assist them. Provide them with valuable resources, expert opinions, or data. By being helpful, you establish your organization as a valuable asset to their work.

Impact: Long-term relationships result in sustained media attention. Journalists are more likely to consider your pitches if they know you and trust your expertise. Long-lasting connections also lead to positive word-of-mouth within the media community.

3. Offer Educational Engagements:

Tip: Expert Interviews: Offer journalists opportunities for expert interviews. Your organization's experts can provide valuable insights on industry trends, research findings, or current events. These interviews position your organization as an authoritative source.

Tip: Workshops and Tours: Organize workshops, seminars, or facility tours tailored to journalists' interests. These educational engagements offer journalists in-depth knowledge about your organization, fostering a deeper understanding and appreciation for your work.

Impact: Educational engagements enhance your relationship with journalists by providing them with unique and enriching experiences. Journalists value organizations that contribute to their professional growth and understanding of various topics.

Additional Tips:

1. **Be Responsive:** Respond promptly to journalists' inquiries, even if you don't have information to share immediately. Acknowledging their queries demonstrates respect for their time and effort.

2. **Express Gratitude:** Show appreciation for media coverage, interviews, or any other support provided by journalists. A simple thank-you note or email goes a long way in building positive relationships.

3. **Respect Deadlines:** Understand journalists' deadlines and respect them. Timely responses to media requests are crucial for maintaining a positive rapport.

4. **Stay Informed:** Keep yourself updated about the media landscape, including journalists' movements, changes in beats, and new publications. Staying informed helps you tailor your pitches effectively.

In summary, successful media relations go beyond transactional interactions. Cultivating trust, focusing on long-term relationships, and offering educational engagements are proactive strategies that lead to enduring partnerships with journalists. By embodying these principles, you not only enhance your organization's media coverage but also contribute positively to the media community. Remember, building meaningful relationships takes time and effort, but the results are invaluable in the world of media relations.

2.8 International Media Relations: Navigating Global Communication

Expanding your media relations internationally brings unique challenges and opportunities. Understanding the nuances of different cultures and tailoring your communication strategies accordingly is essential for successful global outreach. Here's how to effectively engage with international media:

1. Cultural Sensitivity:

Tip: Cross-Cultural Awareness: Familiarize yourself with cultural norms, traditions, and communication styles of the countries you are targeting. Respect for cultural differences is crucial to avoid misunderstandings and misinterpretations.

Tip: Language Considerations: Be mindful of language variations within the same language. For example, American English and British English have subtle differences. Use language that resonates with the specific region's dialect and vocabulary.

Impact: Cultural sensitivity builds trust and rapport with international journalists. Demonstrating an understanding of their cultural context enhances your credibility and fosters positive relationships.

2. Localization:

Tip: Tailor Messages: Customize your messages to align with the cultural and linguistic preferences of the target audience. Localizing content ensures that your message resonates with the local population, making it more relatable and engaging.

Tip: Adapt Visuals: Visual elements, such as images and videos, should also be culturally appropriate. Avoid visuals that could be misinterpreted or deemed insensitive in the target culture.

Impact: Localized messages create a stronger connection with the audience. They are more likely to be well-received and understood, leading to increased acceptance of your organization's narrative.

3. Global Networks:

Tip: Leverage International Partnerships: Collaborate with international media partners and press agencies. These collaborations provide access to their established networks, increasing your visibility on a global scale.

Tip: Utilize Global Platforms: Engage with global platforms and social media channels that have a diverse international audience. Tailor your content to cater to the interests and preferences of users from different countries.

Impact: Leveraging global networks expands your reach significantly. Partnering with international media outlets broadens your exposure, making your organization more recognizable and credible on the global stage.

Additional Considerations:

1. **Legal and Ethical Compliance:** Understand the legal and ethical guidelines related to media communication in each country you target. Adhering to local regulations is crucial to maintain a positive reputation.

2. **Crisis Management:** Have a robust crisis management plan tailored for each region. Cultural perceptions of crises vary; understanding these differences helps in crafting appropriate responses.

3. **Localized Events and Initiatives:** Organize events or initiatives that are relevant to the local community.

Participation in local causes demonstrates your organization's commitment to the region, enhancing your reputation.

In summary, international media relations require a nuanced approach that respects cultural diversity and adapts communication strategies accordingly. By being culturally sensitive, localizing your messages, and leveraging global networks, you can successfully navigate the complexities of international media relations. Building positive relationships with international journalists and audiences not only enhances your global presence but also strengthens your organization's reputation on the international stage. Remember, effective international media relations are built on mutual respect, understanding, and a genuine appreciation for diverse cultures.

2.9 International Media Relations: Navigating Diverse Cultures and Markets

Engaging with international media requires a keen understanding of cultural diversity and a strategic approach to communication. Tailoring your messages, respecting cultural nuances, and leveraging global networks are essential strategies for effective international media relations:

1. Cultural Sensitivity:

Tip: Cultural Research: Invest time in researching the cultural norms, values, and traditions of the countries you are targeting. Understand the nuances of communication, such as formalities, greetings, and taboos.

Tip: Culturally Appropriate Content: Ensure that your content aligns with the cultural values of the target audience. Avoid references or imagery that could be misunderstood or offensive in the cultural context.

Impact: Cultural sensitivity fosters respect and trust. It prevents misunderstandings and demonstrates your organization's awareness and respect for the diversity of global audiences.

2. Localization:

Tip: Language Adaptation: Translate your messages accurately, considering dialects and regional language differences. Use native speakers or professional translators to ensure linguistic nuances are captured effectively.

Tip: Contextual Relevance: Adapt your messaging to align with local customs, holidays, and cultural references. Contextually relevant content resonates more deeply with the audience.

Impact: Localization ensures that your messages are relatable and resonate with the local audience, increasing the likelihood of positive reception and engagement.

3. Global Networks:

Tip: Partnerships and Collaborations: Collaborate with international media outlets, influencers, or organizations. Partnerships provide mutual benefits and expand your reach through shared networks and audiences.

Tip: International Press Agencies: Utilize international press agencies for distribution and syndication. These agencies have established networks, making your stories accessible to a broader audience across various regions.

Impact: Leveraging global networks broadens your exposure and credibility. It helps in reaching diverse markets and demographics, strengthening your organization's global presence.

Additional Considerations:

1. **Crisis Communication:** Have a culturally sensitive crisis communication plan for each region. Understand how crises are perceived and responded to in different cultures to address issues appropriately.

2. **Social and Political Awareness:** Be aware of the social and political landscape in each country. Sensitivity to local issues prevents unintentional controversies and ensures your messaging remains relevant and respectful.

3. **Regular Feedback:** Seek feedback from local representatives or contacts within the target country. Their insights can provide valuable perspectives on the effectiveness of your communication strategies.

4. **Continuous Learning:** Stay updated on global trends, cultural shifts, and international media practices. Continuous learning equips you with the knowledge needed to adapt your strategies effectively.

In summary, international media relations demand a nuanced and culturally sensitive approach. By understanding and respecting diverse cultures, localizing your messages, and leveraging global networks, you can navigate the complexities of international communication successfully. Building strong relationships with international media not only enhances your global reputation but also opens doors to new opportunities and collaborations in diverse markets. Remember, cultural intelligence and adaptability are key to building lasting connections in the global media landscape.

2.10 Monitoring and Evaluation in Media Relations:

Enhancing Strategies through Insightful Analysis

Monitoring and evaluating your media relations efforts are integral components of a successful communication strategy. By employing strategic tools and fostering a feedback-driven approach, you can refine your methods and strengthen your relationships with the media:

1. Media Monitoring:

Tip: Utilize Media Monitoring Tools: Invest in media monitoring software that tracks media coverage, mentions, and sentiment analysis. These tools provide real-time data, allowing you to assess the impact of your media relations efforts.

Tip: Analyze and Refine: Regularly analyze the data gathered from media monitoring. Identify patterns, trends, and the tone of media coverage. Use this information to refine your media pitches, messages, and targeting strategies.

Impact: Media monitoring tools offer valuable insights into your media presence. Analyzing this data enables you to make data-driven decisions, ensuring your efforts align with the evolving media landscape.

2. Feedback Loop:

Tip: Encourage Journalist Feedback: Actively seek feedback from journalists about your interactions. Understand their perspective on your pitches, press releases, and overall engagement. Constructive criticism provides invaluable insights for improvement.

Tip: Engage in Dialogue: Establish open channels of communication where journalists feel comfortable providing feedback. Engage in dialogue, ask for suggestions, and express gratitude for their input. This fosters a collaborative relationship.

Impact: Feedback from journalists offers a unique outside perspective. It highlights areas of improvement, enabling you to enhance your communication techniques. Actively addressing concerns fosters a positive and respectful relationship with the media.

Additional Considerations:

1. **Competitor Analysis:** Monitor media coverage of competitors. Understand their strategies, strengths, and weaknesses. Comparative analysis provides benchmarking opportunities and insights for differentiation.

2. **Impact Assessment:** Evaluate the impact of media coverage on your organization's goals, such as brand awareness, website traffic, or lead generation. Assess how media relations contribute to your overall objectives.

3. **Adaptation to Trends:** Stay informed about media trends, emerging platforms, and changing journalist preferences. Adapt your strategies to align with evolving media practices and audience behaviors.

4. **Regular Reporting:** Develop regular reports summarizing media coverage, sentiment analysis, and feedback received. Share these reports internally to demonstrate the value of media relations efforts and inform strategic decisions.

Monitoring and evaluation are continuous processes that empower your media relations strategies. Media monitoring tools offer insights into your media presence, enabling data-driven decision-making. The feedback loop with journalists fosters open communication and mutual understanding. By embracing these practices, you can adapt, refine, and optimize your media relations efforts, ensuring your organization maintains a positive and impactful presence in the media landscape. Remember, the ability to learn and evolve based on insights is key to building enduring and fruitful relationships with the media.

In summary, successful media relations demand a strategic, personalized, and ethical approach. By conducting thorough research, building genuine relationships, communicating effectively, avoiding common pitfalls, and adapting your strategies for different media contexts, you can establish strong, long-lasting connections with the media at local, national, and international levels. Continuous learning, adaptability, and a genuine passion for storytelling are the foundations of enduring media relations.

Chapter 3: Common Mistakes in Media Relations

In the dynamic landscape of media relations, avoiding common mistakes is essential for building fruitful relationships with journalists and ensuring positive coverage for your organization. Let's delve into each of the mentioned mistakes and discuss strategies to prevent them:

1. Lack of Preparation:

Mistake: Insufficient preparation before engaging with the media.

Solution: Thoroughly prepare for media interactions. Anticipate potential questions, craft key messages, and rehearse responses. Being well-prepared enhances confidence and ensures clear, coherent communication.

Impact: Lack of preparation can lead to vague or inconsistent messaging, weakening your organization's credibility. Adequate preparation establishes you as a reliable and knowledgeable source.

2. Inadequate Research on Journalists and Outlets:

Mistake: Failing to research journalists and media outlets before reaching out.

Solution: Conduct in-depth research on journalists' beats, writing styles, and recent articles. Understand media outlets' focus, audience, and editorial guidelines. Tailor your pitches to align with their interests.

Impact: Inadequate research results in irrelevant pitches, leading to rejections. Tailored pitches based on research increase the likelihood of positive responses.

3. Ignoring Current Events and Trends:

Mistake: Disregarding current events and trends in media pitches.

Solution: Stay informed about current events and industry trends. Align your pitches with relevant topics, showcasing your organization's expertise in real-time issues.

Impact: Ignoring current events makes your pitches appear disconnected and irrelevant. Timely pitches demonstrate relevance and increase journalists' interest.

4. Poor Communication:

Mistake: Ineffective communication methods, unclear messages, or lack of responsiveness.

Solution: Use clear, concise language in all communications. Respond promptly to media inquiries and requests for information. Be professional and respectful in all interactions.

Impact: Poor communication frustrates journalists and damages your organization's reputation. Clear, timely communication fosters positive relationships.

5. Miscommunication with Journalists:

Mistake: Misunderstandings or misinterpretations in communications with journalists.

Solution: Clarify any ambiguities promptly. Seek feedback to ensure mutual understanding. Use precise language to avoid miscommunication.

Impact: Miscommunication erodes trust and may lead to inaccurate or negative coverage. Clear, honest communication promotes positive relationships.

6. Ineffective Pitching Strategies:

Mistake: Generic or unappealing pitches that fail to capture journalists' interest.

Solution: Craft personalized, compelling pitches tailored to each journalist and outlet. Highlight unique angles and benefits relevant to their audience.

Impact: Ineffective pitches are ignored, wasting opportunities for coverage. Engaging pitches capture attention and increase the likelihood of media interest.

7. Overlooking Follow-ups and Relationship Building:

Mistake: Neglecting follow-ups and failing to build ongoing relationships.

Solution: Follow up courteously after sending pitches. Nurture relationships by providing additional resources, story ideas, or expert opinions even when not pitching specific stories.

Impact: Lack of follow-ups results in missed opportunities. Building relationships ensures consistent media interest and coverage.

In the next part, we will continue discussing the remaining mistakes in media relations and explore the importance of visuals, including infographics, images, and videos, in effective communication. Stay tuned for more insights!

8. Ignoring Social Media and Online Presence:

Mistake: Underestimating the impact of social media and online presence in media relations.

Solution: Actively maintain social media profiles with updated information, engaging content, and timely responses. Utilize social media to share news, connect with journalists, and showcase your organization's expertise.

Impact: Ignoring social media limits your reach and engagement. Active online presence amplifies your messages, attracting journalists and enhancing credibility.

9. Neglecting Social Media Platforms:

Mistake: Focusing solely on one social media platform or neglecting emerging platforms.

Solution: Diversify your social media presence across platforms relevant to your target audience. Stay informed about new platforms and assess their suitability for your organization's communication goals.

Impact: Neglecting platforms results in missed opportunities to connect with diverse audiences. Embracing multiple platforms broadens your reach and engages a wider audience.

10. Mishandling Negative Publicity Online:

Mistake: Reacting impulsively or defensively to negative publicity online.

Solution: Address negative comments professionally and constructively. Respond privately if necessary, offering solutions or seeking resolution. Maintain a positive public image and demonstrate willingness to address concerns.

Impact: Mishandling negativity exacerbates the situation, damaging your organization's reputation. Calm, respectful responses showcase professionalism and may mitigate negative perceptions.

11. Expanding Visual Content:

Importance of Visuals: Visual content, such as infographics, images, and videos, enhances the effectiveness of your media relations efforts. Visuals grab attention, simplify complex information, and make stories more memorable.

Incorporating Infographics: Create visually appealing infographics to present data, statistics, or processes. Infographics are easily shareable and digestible, making complex information accessible to a broader audience.

Utilizing Images and Videos: Include high-quality images and videos in press releases and media pitches. Visual assets provide context, evoke emotions, and make stories more compelling. Videos can feature interviews, behind-the-scenes footage, or demonstrations, adding depth to your narratives.

Impact of Visual Content: Visuals capture audience interest, increasing the likelihood of media coverage. Journalists often prefer visually rich stories, as they resonate better with readers and viewers, amplifying your message effectively.

Incorporating these strategies and avoiding common mistakes in media relations enhances your organization's reputation, strengthens relationships with journalists, and maximizes positive media coverage. By embracing effective communication, thorough research, and visual storytelling, you can navigate the media landscape successfully, ensuring your messages resonate with audiences worldwide. Remember, each interaction is an opportunity to build lasting connections and shape public perception positively.

Chapter 4: Media Relations Tips and Best Practices

In this chapter, we will explore essential tips and best practices in media relations. These strategies, ranging from research and effective communication to relationship-building and interactive elements, are designed to empower readers in applying media relations strategies successfully in real-world scenarios.

1. Research and Targeting:

Tip: Understanding Media Outlets:

Researching various media outlets is the foundation of effective media relations. Each outlet has a unique audience, tone, and content preference. Understanding these aspects is key to tailoring your pitches successfully. Aligning your pitches with each outlet's unique style and focus significantly increases your chances of grabbing journalists' attention and securing media coverage.

Explanation:

Why Understanding Media Outlets Matters: Different media outlets cater to diverse audiences. For instance, a lifestyle magazine targets readers interested in fashion, travel, and entertainment, while a tech blog focuses on innovations and gadgets. Tailoring your message to resonate with the specific interests of each outlet ensures that your story aligns with what their audience finds relevant and engaging.

Example: Suppose you represent a sustainable fashion brand launching a new eco-friendly clothing line. Here's how you might tailor your pitch for two different media outlets:

1. **For a Fashion Magazine (Target Audience: Trendy Consumers):**

   - **Tailored Pitch:** "Elevate Your Style Ethically: Discover [Your Brand Name]'s Latest Eco-Friendly Collection!"

   - **Content Emphasis:** Focus on the fashionable aspects of the clothing line, highlighting chic designs, celebrity endorsements (if any), and how the eco-friendly materials are trendy and stylish.

2. **For an Environmental Sustainability Blog (Target Audience: Eco-conscious Consumers):**

   - **Tailored Pitch:** "Fashioning a Greener Future: Unveiling [Your Brand Name]'s Sustainable Clothing Line!"

   - **Content Emphasis:** Emphasize the eco-friendly aspects, detailing the materials used, the brand's commitment to sustainability, and how the clothing line contributes to reducing the fashion industry's carbon footprint.

By tailoring your pitch according to each outlet's focus, you speak directly to the interests of their readership. This personalized approach significantly enhances the likelihood of your story being considered for publication. Understanding the unique nuances of media outlets ensures your message resonates effectively, making your media relations efforts more impactful and successful.

2. Effective Communication:

Tip 1: Mastering Email Pitching:

Explanation:

Email pitching is a fundamental aspect of media relations, often serving as the first point of contact between you and a journalist. Crafting compelling email pitches requires precision and creativity. Journalists receive numerous emails daily; therefore, your pitch must stand out from the rest. Here's how to master email pitching:

- **Concise and Engaging:** Craft your email pitch to be concise yet engaging. Journalists don't have time for lengthy emails. Clearly and succinctly outline the core of your story within the first few lines. Use language that captivates and sparks curiosity.

- **Relevance and Importance:** Clearly state the relevance of your story to the journalist's beat and their audience. Explain why your story matters and how it addresses current trends, issues, or interests. Make it evident why their readers or viewers would find the story compelling.

Example:

Subject Line: "Revolutionizing Sustainable Agriculture: [Your Company Name]'s Breakthrough in Organic Farming"

Email Body: Hi [Journalist's Name],

I hope this email finds you well. I am writing to introduce you to an exciting development in the realm of sustainable agriculture. [Your Company Name] has recently pioneered a groundbreaking organic farming technique that not only enhances crop yield but also promotes soil health without the use of harmful chemicals.

Our story delves into the journey of local farmers who have adopted this method, their successes, and the positive environmental impact of this approach. In a world increasingly concerned about food security and eco-conscious living, we believe this story would resonate profoundly with your readers at [Media Outlet Name].

I have attached a press release with more details and high-resolution images. I would be happy to provide additional information or facilitate an interview with our expert, Dr. [Expert's Name], at your convenience.

Thank you for your time. I look forward to the possibility of collaborating on this impactful narrative.

Best regards, [Your Full Name] [Your Position] [Your Company] [Your Email Address] [Your Phone Number]

Tip 2: Building Relationships:

Explanation:

Building and nurturing relationships with journalists go beyond transactional interactions. Long-term relationships are built on trust, reliability, and mutual respect. Here's how to foster these relationships effectively:

- **Active Engagement:** Beyond pitch emails, engage with journalists on social media platforms. Comment on their articles, share their work, and participate in discussions related to their field. Genuine engagement demonstrates your interest in their work.

- **Attend Industry Events:** Actively participate in industry events, conferences, and seminars where journalists are present. Face-to-face interactions provide opportunities to establish rapport and learn more about their interests and reporting styles.

- **Offer Assistance:** Be proactive in offering assistance even when you are not pitching stories. If you come across information or sources that might be relevant to their beat, share it without expecting anything in return. This helpful attitude strengthens your relationship.

Example:

Imagine you find an article by a journalist you've been following, discussing challenges faced by local farmers in the face of climate change.

Social Media Engagement: You could comment on the article, expressing your appreciation for shedding light on this important issue. You might also share the article on your social media platforms, tagging the journalist and acknowledging their insightful reporting.

Direct Outreach: In a follow-up email, you could say, "I recently came across your article on the challenges faced by local farmers. I found it incredibly insightful. If you ever need additional perspectives or data on sustainable farming practices, please feel free to reach out. I'm here to assist in any way I can."

By consistently engaging, showing genuine interest, and offering support, you demonstrate your commitment to building a meaningful, long-lasting relationship with the journalist.

By mastering email pitching and building relationships, you establish yourself as a reliable and valuable resource for journalists. These practices not only enhance your chances of securing media coverage but also contribute to fostering a positive and mutually beneficial relationship with the media professionals you collaborate with.

3. Handling Media Interviews and Press Conferences:

Tip 1: Media Training:

Explanation:

Media interviews can be intense and unpredictable. Proper training ensures that your spokespeople are well-prepared to handle various situations. Media training equips them with essential skills such as maintaining message consistency, handling tough questions tactfully, and staying composed under pressure. This training helps in conveying your organization's narrative effectively while addressing challenging inquiries.

Example:

Consider your organization is launching a new technology product. During media training, your spokesperson could be coached on:

- **Message Consistency:** Ensuring that key messages about the product's unique features, benefits, and impact are consistently communicated in every interview.

- **Handling Tough Questions:** Training your spokesperson to address potentially difficult questions. For instance, if the product faced criticism about its environmental impact, the spokesperson should be prepared to discuss your organization's sustainability initiatives and plans for improvement.

- **Maintaining Composure:** Teaching techniques to remain calm and composed, even when faced with aggressive or confrontational interviewers. Techniques such as active listening and taking a moment to gather thoughts before responding can be invaluable.

Tip 2: Effective Press Conferences:

Explanation:

Press conferences are high-profile events where your organization's announcements are made to the media and, consequently, the public. Effective planning and execution are crucial. A well-organized press conference includes a clear agenda, engaging visuals or presentations, and opportunities for journalists to ask questions. Post-event, timely follow-ups with relevant resources, additional information, or clarification further reinforce your message.

Example:

Suppose your organization is unveiling a groundbreaking environmental initiative. Here's how you might plan and execute a press conference:

- **Clear Agenda:** Outline the key points that will be covered during the conference. For instance, the agenda could include the initiative's goals, implementation plan, expected impact, and how the community can get involved.

- **Engaging Visuals:** Prepare compelling visuals such as infographics, charts, and videos that visually represent the initiative's impact and benefits. Visuals make complex information accessible and memorable.

- **Interactive Session:** Dedicate a portion of the conference for journalists to ask questions. Allow them to engage directly with your experts or spokespeople. Be prepared to provide detailed and transparent answers, reinforcing your organization's commitment to openness.

- **Follow-up Resources:** After the conference, promptly send out a press kit containing high-resolution images, detailed information about the initiative, expert quotes, and contact information for further inquiries. This additional information helps journalists craft accurate and comprehensive stories.

By providing media training to your spokespeople and executing press conferences effectively, your organization not only ensures a coherent and positive representation but also maximizes the impact of your announcements. These practices contribute to building a strong and credible media presence, fostering trust with both journalists and the wider audience.

4. Interactive Elements:

Introduction of Exercises and Worksheets:

Explanation:

Incorporating interactive elements like exercises and worksheets into your media relations materials transforms passive reading into active learning experiences. These tools serve as practical guides, allowing readers to apply media relations strategies to real-world scenarios. Exercises might involve crafting sample pitches, developing media communication plans, or analyzing case studies. Worksheets provide structured formats for organizing information, helping readers to refine their messaging and communication strategies.

Example:

Let's consider a hypothetical scenario where a company is conducting a media relations workshop. As part of the workshop materials, an exercise could involve:

Exercise: Crafting a Pitch for a Fictitious Product Launch

Background: Participants are provided with a fictitious product—a revolutionary smartphone app that enhances mental well-being through guided meditation and stress-relief techniques.

Task: Participants are asked to craft a pitch email targeting a lifestyle magazine, emphasizing the app's unique features, user benefits, and its relevance to the magazine's audience.

Worksheet:

1. Target Audience: Identify the primary readership of the lifestyle magazine. What are their interests, age group, and lifestyle choices?

2. Key App Features: List the distinctive features of the mental well-being app. What sets it apart from other meditation apps? What benefits does it offer to users?

3. Crafting the Pitch: Draft a concise and engaging pitch email to the magazine's lifestyle editor. Ensure the email clearly communicates the app's benefits and why it would resonate with the magazine's readership.

Impact of Interactive Learning:

Enhanced Engagement and Retention: Interactive elements like exercises and worksheets encourage active participation. Readers engage with the material, analyzing, and synthesizing information. This hands-on approach fosters a deeper understanding of media relations concepts.

Practical Application: By simulating real-world scenarios, readers can directly apply what they learn. Crafting pitches, conducting mock media interviews, and evaluating case studies enable them to hone their skills, preparing them for actual media interactions.

Skill Development: Through interactive learning, readers develop practical skills such as effective messaging, media outreach, and crisis communication. These skills are invaluable for navigating the complexities of media relations in various contexts.

By incorporating interactive elements, you create an immersive learning experience. Readers not only absorb theoretical knowledge but also practice and refine their skills, ensuring they are well-prepared and confident when facing real media relations challenges. Interactive learning transforms passive readers into active participants, empowering them to excel in the dynamic field of media relations.

By implementing these tips and best practices, readers can enhance their media relations skills, build lasting relationships with journalists, and secure positive media coverage for their organizations. These practical strategies, coupled with interactive learning experiences, provide a comprehensive approach to mastering the art of media relations in today's dynamic and competitive media landscape. Remember, media relations is not just a transactional process; it's about building enduring relationships and effectively communicating your organization's story to the world.

Chapter 5: Case Studies in Media Relations

Successful Media Relations Campaigns (1)

Media relations case studies offer valuable insights into successful strategies, execution, and results achieved by organizations. Analyzing real-world examples provides actionable takeaways for improving your own media relations efforts. In this chapter, we will delve into a specific case study to understand the intricacies of a successful media relations campaign.

Case Study 1: XYZ Company's Product Launch Campaign

Background: XYZ Company, a leading tech innovator, was set to launch its revolutionary smart home device, aiming to transform how people interacted with their living spaces.

Strategy: XYZ Company's media relations team meticulously planned the campaign. They identified key media outlets catering to technology enthusiasts, home decor aficionados, and lifestyle bloggers. The team crafted tailored pitches for each outlet, emphasizing different aspects of the smart home device, such as its cutting-edge technology, aesthetic design, and user-friendly interface. Personalized emails were sent out to journalists, inviting them to an exclusive product launch event.

Execution: The launch event was a meticulously curated experience. Journalists and influencers were given hands-on demonstrations of the smart home device's features. Engaging visuals and interactive displays showcased its capabilities. XYZ Company's CEO and product developers were available for interviews, providing in-depth insights into the technology and its development process. Press kits containing high-resolution images, press releases, and detailed specifications were distributed.

Results: The media coverage was extensive and positive. XYZ Company's product launch was featured in prominent tech blogs, lifestyle magazines, and major news outlets. Influencers shared their experiences on social media platforms, generating buzz and anticipation among consumers. The campaign resulted in a significant increase in pre-orders and brand visibility. XYZ Company received positive reviews, and the smart home device gained a strong foothold in the market.

Key Takeaways:

1. **Targeted Outreach:** Identifying and targeting media outlets catering to specific audience segments ensured that the product reached the right audience, maximizing impact.

2. **Personalized Pitches:** Tailoring pitches for each outlet highlighted the aspects most likely to resonate with their readers, increasing the likelihood of coverage.

3. **Engaging Events:** The interactive and engaging launch event provided journalists with a memorable experience, making them more likely to cover the product in their publications.

4. **Availability of Resources:** Providing comprehensive press kits and access to key company figures facilitated accurate and in-depth reporting, ensuring the message was communicated effectively.

5. **Influencer Engagement:** Involving influencers amplified the campaign's reach, leveraging their followers and credibility to create additional buzz around the product.

By analyzing the successful media relations campaign of XYZ Company, we learn the importance of strategic planning, personalized communication, engaging events, and leveraging influencers. These strategies can be applied to future media relations efforts, enhancing the likelihood of achieving impactful and positive results.

Case Study 2: ABC Non-Profit Organization's Awareness Campaign

Background: ABC Non-Profit Organization, dedicated to environmental conservation, aimed to raise awareness about the importance of sustainable living practices and the impact of climate change on local communities. Their goal was to engage a wide audience, from students to policymakers, to inspire collective action for a greener future.

Outreach: ABC Non-Profit Organization identified various stakeholders, including schools, local businesses, community leaders, and environmental influencers. The media relations team crafted a compelling narrative emphasizing the urgency of environmental preservation and the tangible steps individuals and communities could take. Outreach efforts involved targeted emails, social media campaigns, and personalized phone calls to key influencers and journalists.

Engagement: To engage the community, ABC Non-Profit Organization organized interactive workshops, tree planting events, and educational seminars in collaboration with local schools and businesses. They created visually appealing educational materials, including infographics and short videos, explaining the impact of climate change on the region. Volunteers and staff actively engaged with attendees, encouraging them to share their experiences on social media using a dedicated hashtag.

Media Coverage: Local and regional media outlets were engaged through press releases, emphasizing the urgency of the cause and the organization's innovative approach to environmental education. ABC Non-Profit Organization facilitated interviews with their experts and community members affected by climate change. High-quality visuals, such as before-and-after images of reforested areas, were provided to the media, enhancing the visual appeal of the story.

Results: The campaign garnered extensive media coverage in local newspapers, television channels, and online platforms. Influencers and community leaders actively participated, amplifying the message across social media. The hashtag associated with the campaign trended locally, reaching a broad audience. Public participation in workshops and events increased significantly, leading to a surge in new memberships and volunteer sign-ups for ABC Non-Profit Organization.

Key Takeaways:

1. **Community Engagement:** Actively involving the community in events and workshops fosters a sense of ownership, making individuals more likely to support and promote the cause.

2. **Compelling Visuals:** High-quality images and videos depicting the impact of climate change and the organization's efforts make the campaign more visually appealing and shareable.

3. **Partnerships and Collaborations:** Partnering with local schools, businesses, and influencers extends the campaign's reach and credibility, tapping into existing networks.

4. **Digital Storytelling:** Leveraging social media and multimedia formats allows for impactful storytelling,

enabling the organization to connect with a broader and more diverse audience.

5. **Measurable Impact:** Showcasing tangible outcomes, such as reforested areas, demonstrates the organization's effectiveness, inspiring confidence among supporters and the media.

By strategically employing outreach, engagement, and media coverage, ABC Non-Profit Organization successfully elevated awareness about their cause. Their holistic approach, combining community involvement, digital outreach, and compelling narratives, serves as a model for future non-profit awareness campaigns.

Case Study 3: XYZ Political Campaign's Grassroots Mobilization

Background: XYZ Political Campaign, aiming to secure a seat in a highly contested local election, focused on grassroots mobilization. Their goal was to engage with diverse communities, address their concerns, and establish a strong voter base. The campaign's success hinged on effective media relations to convey their candidate's vision and connect with voters on a personal level.

Strategy: XYZ Political Campaign devised a multifaceted media relations strategy. They identified key issues concerning local residents and formulated clear, concise messages addressing these concerns. The campaign team conducted in-depth research on local media outlets, including community newspapers, radio stations, and influential social media influencers. Personalized press releases were crafted for each outlet, highlighting the candidate's stance on local issues.

Grassroots Engagement: The campaign organized town hall meetings, neighborhood gatherings, and door-to-door outreach initiatives. At these events, the candidate actively listened to residents' concerns, providing empathetic responses. The campaign team documented these interactions, transforming them into compelling narratives for the media. Grassroots volunteers were trained to engage effectively, ensuring a consistent message reached voters.

Media Outreach: The campaign maintained a strong social media presence, sharing regular updates, policy insights, and behind-the-scenes glimpses of the candidate's activities. They actively engaged with local journalists on social platforms, showcasing the candidate's accessibility and willingness to engage with the media. Additionally, XYZ Political Campaign offered exclusive interviews and expert commentary to local news outlets, positioning the candidate as a thought leader on key local issues.

Community Partnerships: Recognizing the importance of endorsements, the campaign sought partnerships with respected community leaders, local businesses, and influential organizations. Endorsement events were held, generating media coverage and reinforcing the candidate's credibility. Collaborations with grassroots activists and local nonprofits amplified the campaign's reach and authenticity, fostering trust within the community.

Results: XYZ Political Campaign's grassroots mobilization efforts garnered widespread media coverage. Local newspapers featured stories about the candidate's interactions with residents, highlighting their genuine concern for the community. Radio interviews and podcasts allowed the candidate to delve into nuanced policy discussions. Social media engagement skyrocketed, with posts and videos reaching thousands of local residents. The endorsements from community leaders and organizations added significant credibility, influencing undecided voters.

Key Takeaways:

1. **Authentic Engagement:** Genuine, empathetic interactions with voters, documented and shared with the media, establish a deep connection, making the candidate relatable and trustworthy.

2. **Strategic Media Partnerships:** Tailoring messages for diverse media outlets and engaging journalists directly ensure the campaign's narrative reaches varied demographics.

3. **Social Media Amplification:** Leveraging social media platforms for real-time updates, policy discussions, and

community engagement enhances visibility and fosters a sense of community.

4. **Endorsements and Credibility:** Partnerships with respected community figures and organizations bolster the campaign's credibility, influencing public opinion.

5. **Consistent Messaging:** Maintaining consistency in messages across all platforms and interactions solidifies the candidate's image and fosters a sense of reliability among voters.

By executing a comprehensive media relations campaign grounded in genuine community engagement, strategic media outreach, and credible endorsements, XYZ Political Campaign successfully connected with voters. This approach not only increased visibility but also established a lasting rapport, essential for any successful political campaign.

Case Study 4: GreenEarth Initiative's Environmental Awareness Drive

Background: GreenEarth Initiative, a non-governmental organization dedicated to environmental conservation, launched a comprehensive media relations campaign to raise awareness about pressing environmental issues and promote sustainable practices. Their objective was to mobilize communities, garner support for conservation efforts, and influence policy changes at both local and national levels.

Strategy: GreenEarth Initiative designed a multifaceted media relations strategy encompassing traditional and digital channels. They identified key environmental challenges such as deforestation, plastic pollution, and climate change. The campaign team collaborated with environmental experts, scientists, and influential personalities to create evidence-based narratives. The strategy focused on educating the public, advocating for policy changes, and encouraging individuals and businesses to adopt eco-friendly practices.

Media Outreach: GreenEarth Initiative engaged with a wide array of media outlets, including television networks, radio stations, environmental blogs, and social media platforms. They crafted compelling press releases, emphasizing the urgency of the environmental issues and presenting viable solutions. Engaging visuals, such as infographics, videos, and before-and-after photographs, were created to illustrate the impact of environmental degradation.

Community Engagement: The organization organized tree-planting drives, beach clean-ups, and educational workshops in schools and communities. These events were widely publicized through local newspapers and social media. Interactive sessions and seminars were conducted, featuring renowned environmentalists and scientists, encouraging active participation and knowledge sharing.

Policy Advocacy: GreenEarth Initiative collaborated with lawmakers, organizing press conferences and panel discussions to advocate for eco-friendly policies and legislation. The organization provided journalists with well-researched policy briefs, emphasizing the potential positive impact of proposed environmental regulations on communities and the planet.

Results: The campaign generated substantial media coverage across various platforms. Television networks aired documentaries featuring GreenEarth Initiative's conservation projects. Radio programs highlighted interviews with experts, encouraging listeners to adopt sustainable practices. Newspapers featured success stories from community-led initiatives, and social media engagement soared, with hashtags associated with the campaign trending nationally. As a result of the campaign's advocacy efforts, several local governments implemented plastic reduction policies, and businesses pledged to reduce their carbon footprint.

Key Takeaways:

1. **Evidence-Based Narratives:** Backing campaigns with scientific data and expert opinions lends credibility and persuasiveness to the message.

2. **Multichannel Approach:** Leveraging diverse media outlets ensures the message reaches different demographics, maximizing impact.

3. **Community Involvement:** Engaging communities through interactive events fosters a sense of ownership,

encouraging active participation and long-term commitment to the cause.

4. **Policy Advocacy:** Collaborating with policymakers and providing well-researched policy recommendations can lead to tangible legislative changes.

5. **Measurable Impact:** Highlighting the concrete outcomes of environmental initiatives showcases the organization's effectiveness, inspiring confidence and support from the public and stakeholders.

Through their media relations campaign, GreenEarth Initiative not only raised awareness about environmental issues but also catalyzed real change at the community and policy levels. Their strategic and comprehensive approach serves as a model for other environmental organizations aiming to make a meaningful impact on conservation efforts.

Case Study 5: Embassy of Serenity - Promoting Cultural Diplomacy

Background: The Embassy of Serenity, a country renowned for its rich cultural heritage and scenic beauty, embarked on a strategic media relations campaign to promote cultural diplomacy, attract tourists, and foster international collaborations. Their goal was to create a positive and nuanced image of Serenity, showcasing its diverse traditions, culinary delights, art, and natural wonders.

Strategy: The Embassy of Serenity crafted a meticulous media relations strategy focusing on highlighting the country's unique cultural offerings. They collaborated with travel influencers, renowned chefs, artists, and historians from both Serenity and around the world. The campaign aimed to build bridges between Serenity and other nations, emphasizing mutual respect and understanding through cultural exchange.

Media Partnerships: The embassy formed partnerships with influential travel magazines, TV networks, and online platforms. They organized familiarization trips for international journalists, bloggers, and television crews, allowing them to experience Serenity's cultural marvels firsthand. These media professionals were encouraged to immerse themselves in local traditions, cuisines, and artistic expressions, enabling them to share authentic and compelling narratives.

Virtual Reality Experience: To provide a unique and immersive experience, the embassy developed a virtual reality (VR) tour of Serenity's historical sites, museums, and natural landscapes. They distributed VR headsets to international media outlets, enabling audiences worldwide to explore Serenity from the comfort of their homes. This innovative approach captured the imagination of viewers and offered a tantalizing glimpse into the country's allure.

Culinary Diplomacy: The embassy organized culinary events featuring Serenity's renowned chefs. They conducted cooking workshops, inviting local chefs to share their expertise and traditional recipes. International food bloggers and journalists were invited to these events, creating a buzz around Serenity's culinary heritage. Recipes and cooking demonstrations were shared through social media, engaging food enthusiasts globally.

Results: The media campaign generated extensive international coverage, with travel features, documentaries, and articles showcasing Serenity's culture, landscapes, and traditions. The virtual reality tour received millions of views, sparking curiosity and inspiring travel plans. Culinary diplomacy events led to collaborations between Serenity's and foreign chefs, creating fusion dishes that gained popularity worldwide. Tourist footfall increased significantly, contributing to the country's economy, while collaborations in the arts, cuisine, and academia flourished.

Key Takeaways:

1. **Collaborative Storytelling:** Partnering with influencers and professionals from diverse fields enriches the narrative, providing varied perspectives and engaging a broader audience.

2. **Immersive Experiences:** Embracing innovative technologies like virtual reality enhances engagement, offering audiences an immersive and memorable experience.

3. **Culinary Diplomacy:** Food events and collaborations create a tangible connection with people, inviting them to explore culture through taste and aroma, fostering cultural understanding.

4. **Authenticity and Respect:** Emphasizing authenticity and respecting local traditions are crucial, ensuring that the portrayal of Serenity resonates with both the local population and international audiences.

5. **Long-term Partnerships:** Building lasting relationships with media outlets and influencers fosters ongoing positive coverage and collaborations, sustaining the positive image of the country.

The Embassy of Serenity's media relations campaign exemplifies the power of cultural diplomacy, showcasing the country's unique heritage and forging meaningful international connections. By focusing on immersive experiences, collaborative storytelling, and culinary diplomacy, they successfully enhanced Serenity's global image, fostering a spirit of mutual respect and curiosity among people worldwide.

Case Study 6: Guardian Hearts - Protecting Families, Empowering Children

Background: Guardian Hearts, a non-profit organization dedicated to safeguarding family values, children, and youth from abuse and drug-related issues, initiated a comprehensive media relations campaign. Their objective was to raise awareness about the importance of a nurturing family environment, educate

83

communities on recognizing signs of abuse, and empower children with the knowledge and resources to protect themselves from substance abuse and exploitation.

Strategy: Guardian Hearts devised a multifaceted media relations strategy focusing on prevention, education, and community engagement. They collaborated with child psychologists, educators, law enforcement agencies, and renowned child advocates. The campaign aimed to address the root causes of abuse and drug-related problems while fostering a supportive environment for families.

Media Partnerships: The organization partnered with television networks, radio stations, and social media influencers known for their commitment to social causes. They developed compelling public service announcements (PSAs) featuring testimonials from survivors, expert advice, and success stories of children overcoming challenges. These PSAs were aired during prime time slots, reaching a broad audience and encouraging conversations about family values and child protection.

School Outreach Programs: Guardian Hearts conducted interactive workshops and seminars in schools nationwide. These programs focused on teaching children about personal boundaries, recognizing inappropriate behavior, and building self-confidence. Educational materials, including age-appropriate booklets, videos, and games, were distributed to schools, encouraging teachers and parents to engage in open discussions with children about sensitive topics.

Community Engagement: The organization organized community events, including family fun days, sports tournaments, and art exhibitions, with a focus on promoting healthy family interactions. Local celebrities and influencers endorsed these events, drawing large crowds. At these gatherings, Guardian Hearts set up information booths staffed by counselors and psychologists who provided guidance to parents and children. Interactive activities for children, such as art projects and games, reinforced the importance of family values.

Helpline and Online Support: Guardian Hearts established a 24/7 helpline manned by trained counselors, psychologists, and legal experts. They also launched a user-friendly website and mobile app offering resources, articles, and videos addressing various aspects of family values, child protection, and substance abuse prevention. The online platform allowed users to anonymously seek advice, ensuring confidentiality and support for those in need.

Results: The media campaign generated substantial coverage across television, radio, and social media platforms. Public service announcements reached millions of viewers, prompting discussions within families about child protection and the importance of nurturing family environments. School outreach programs educated thousands of children, equipping them with knowledge and confidence to protect themselves. Community events fostered a sense of belonging and unity, strengthening family bonds. The helpline and online platform provided immediate support to individuals facing challenges, guiding them toward appropriate resources and assistance.

Key Takeaways:

1. **Collaborative Expertise:** Partnering with psychologists, educators, and law enforcement agencies ensures the campaign's information is accurate, credible, and empathetic.

2. **Interactive Education:** Engaging children in interactive workshops and activities fosters a deeper understanding of sensitive topics, encouraging open communication with parents and educators.

3. **Community Involvement:** Organizing community events and involving local influencers create a sense of shared responsibility, reinforcing the message of family values and child protection.

4. **Accessible Support:** Establishing helplines and online platforms provides immediate support and resources to individuals in need, ensuring help is accessible and confidential.

5. **Continued Engagement:** Sustaining the campaign through ongoing workshops, events, and online support ensures that the message of family values and

child protection remains prominent in the community's consciousness.

Guardian Hearts' media relations campaign exemplifies a holistic approach to protecting families and empowering children. By combining expert knowledge, community engagement, and accessible support, they successfully created a supportive environment where families are educated, children are empowered, and everyone is encouraged to embrace and protect family values.

Failed Media Relations Attempts:

Case Study 1: Failed Product Launch by Company Z

Background: Company Z, a tech startup, aimed to launch a revolutionary product that had the potential to transform the market. They had invested heavily in research, development, and production, believing they had a groundbreaking solution. However, their product launch turned into a significant failure, resulting in low sales, negative media coverage, and damaged brand reputation.

Analyzing Mistakes and Lessons Learned:

1. **Lack of Clear Messaging:**

   - **Mistake:** Company Z failed to communicate the unique selling points and benefits of their product clearly. Their messaging was vague and lacked a compelling narrative.

- **Lesson Learned:** Clear and concise messaging is essential. Companies must articulate what sets their product apart and how it addresses consumers' needs. Crafting a compelling story helps capture media and consumer interest.

2. **Insufficient Media Outreach:**

- **Mistake:** Company Z did not conduct adequate media outreach before the launch. They failed to engage tech journalists, bloggers, or influencers who could have created buzz around their product.

- **Lesson Learned:** Building relationships with relevant media outlets and influencers is crucial. Engaging with the right audience can generate anticipation and positive coverage before the launch, ensuring a successful reception.

3. **Overlooking Product Testing:**

- **Mistake:** Company Z did not conduct thorough product testing and failed to address initial glitches. As a result, the product faced negative reviews and criticisms upon its release.

- **Lesson Learned:** Rigorous testing and addressing issues beforehand are essential. Quality assurance ensures that the product functions as advertised, preventing negative reviews and customer dissatisfaction.

4. **Ignoring Feedback and Reviews:**

- **Mistake:** Company Z ignored negative feedback and reviews from early users. They did not respond to customer complaints or attempt to improve the product based on this feedback.

- **Lesson Learned:** Listening to customer feedback is critical. Addressing concerns promptly demonstrates a commitment to customer satisfaction and can mitigate negative sentiment.

5. **Mismanaged Crisis Communication:**

- **Mistake:** When negative reviews and criticisms started circulating, Company Z responded defensively and dismissively, exacerbating the situation.

- **Lesson Learned:** Effective crisis communication is vital. Companies should respond promptly, empathetically, and professionally to address concerns. Acknowledging issues and outlining steps for improvement can help regain public trust.

6. **Inadequate Preparation for Media Interviews:**

- **Mistake:** Company Z representatives were not adequately prepared for media interviews. Their lack of confidence and inconsistent responses led to further skepticism about the product.

- **Lesson Learned:** Media training is essential. Spokespersons should be well-prepared, confident, and capable of conveying key messages clearly. Training ensures that representatives can handle tough questions and present the company in a positive light.

7. **Failure to Leverage Social Media:**

- **Mistake:** Company Z neglected social media platforms, missing opportunities to engage with potential customers and address concerns directly.

- **Lesson Learned:** Social media is a powerful tool for customer engagement and feedback. Companies should actively participate in conversations, respond to inquiries, and utilize social media platforms to build a loyal customer base and address concerns.

Conclusion: Company Z's failed product launch serves as a stark reminder of the importance of clear messaging, media outreach, product testing, customer feedback, crisis communication, spokesperson preparedness, and social media engagement. By learning from these mistakes, companies can approach their media relations efforts with a more strategic and prepared mindset, increasing their chances of a successful product launch and positive brand perception.

Case Study 2: Public Relations Crisis at Organization Y:

Identifying Errors and Recovery Strategies

Background:

Organization Y, a prominent entity in its industry, faced a severe public relations crisis that threatened its reputation and stakeholder trust. The crisis stemmed from a series of missteps, leading to negative media coverage, public outrage, and a decline in investor confidence. The organization found itself at the center of a storm, requiring swift and strategic action to mitigate the damage and regain public trust.

Identifying Errors:

1. **Lack of Transparency:**

   - **Error:** Organization Y was perceived as non-transparent, withholding crucial information from the public and stakeholders regarding the crisis, which fueled speculation and distrust.

   - **Recovery Strategy:** Adopt a policy of radical transparency. Acknowledge mistakes, disclose relevant information, and communicate openly with stakeholders. Transparency builds credibility and fosters trust.

2. **Delayed Response:**

- **Error:** Organization Y's response to the crisis was delayed, allowing negative narratives to dominate public discourse and leaving stakeholders feeling unheard and undervalued.

- **Recovery Strategy:** Respond swiftly and proactively to crises. Develop a crisis communication plan that includes designated spokespersons, clear messaging, and a rapid response team. Address concerns promptly to prevent the escalation of negative sentiment.

3. **Inadequate Crisis Management Team:**

- **Error:** Organization Y lacked a dedicated crisis management team, leading to disorganized and inconsistent communication during the crisis.

- **Recovery Strategy:** Establish a crisis management team comprising experienced communicators, legal advisors, and key executives. Conduct regular crisis drills and simulations to prepare the team for various scenarios, ensuring a coordinated and effective response.

4. **Insensitive Communication:**

- **Error:** The communication from Organization Y was perceived as insensitive, lacking empathy and understanding of the concerns and emotions of the affected stakeholders.

- **Recovery Strategy:** Cultivate empathy and compassion in communication. Acknowledge the emotional impact of the crisis on stakeholders. Craft messages that demonstrate understanding and convey a genuine commitment to addressing concerns and rectifying the situation.

5. **Neglecting Social Media and Online Platforms:**

- **Error:** Organization Y did not actively engage with stakeholders on social media platforms, allowing negative narratives to thrive unchecked in the digital sphere.

- **Recovery Strategy:** Leverage social media and online platforms to disseminate accurate information, address concerns, and engage with stakeholders directly. Monitor online conversations and respond promptly to mitigate misinformation and negativity.

Recovery Strategies:

1. **Open and Honest Apology:**

- Organization Y should issue a sincere public apology, acknowledging the mistakes made and expressing genuine remorse. An open admission of fault demonstrates accountability and can foster forgiveness.

2. **Engage with Stakeholders:**

   - Actively engage with affected stakeholders, including customers, employees, and investors. Conduct town hall meetings, webinars, and focus groups to listen to their concerns, answer questions, and rebuild relationships.

3. **Implement Reforms:**

   - Institute internal reforms and transparent processes to prevent similar issues in the future. Communicate these reforms to the public, demonstrating a commitment to change and improvement.

4. **Positive Narrative Building:**

   - Develop and disseminate positive stories about Organization Y's contributions to the community, industry, and society. Highlighting positive aspects can balance the negative narrative and restore public faith.

5. **Media Training:**

   - Provide media training to key spokespersons to ensure consistent and empathetic communication. Training should focus on handling tough questions, demonstrating empathy, and conveying the organization's commitment to rectifying the situation.

6. **Long-Term Reputation Management:**

- Develop a long-term reputation management strategy that involves ongoing engagement with stakeholders, transparent communication, and proactive measures to prevent future crises. Building a resilient reputation requires continuous effort and commitment.

By acknowledging past errors, implementing strategic recovery strategies, and adopting a proactive approach to reputation management, Organization Y can navigate the crisis, rebuild trust, and emerge stronger, demonstrating resilience and integrity to its stakeholders.

Case Study 3: Failed Media Relations Attempt in Political Crisis

Background:

In a politically charged environment, Country X's ruling party faced a significant crisis due to a controversial policy decision. The government's media relations strategy in handling the crisis was marred by missteps, resulting in widespread public outrage, international condemnation, and a significant drop in popularity.

Identifying Errors:

1. **Suppressive Tactics:**

    - **Error:** The government resorted to suppressive tactics, including censorship and arrests of journalists critical of the policy. These actions fueled public resentment and intensified media scrutiny.

    - **Recovery Strategy:** Respect freedom of the press and freedom of speech. Embrace open dialogue and engage with journalists, addressing their concerns and clarifying the government's stance.

2. **Misleading Information:**

    - **Error:** Misleading information was disseminated through official channels, leading to confusion and mistrust among the public and international community.

    - **Recovery Strategy:** Uphold truthfulness and transparency. Provide accurate information through credible sources to regain public trust and credibility on the international stage.

3. **Lack of International Communication:**

    - **Error:** The government failed to engage in constructive international communication, leading to negative global perceptions and strained diplomatic relations.

- **Recovery Strategy:** Foster international understanding through diplomatic channels. Communicate the government's perspective effectively, addressing concerns and seeking common ground with international stakeholders.

4. **Failure to Address Concerns:**

- **Error:** Instead of addressing citizens' concerns, the government dismissed public sentiment, further alienating the population.

- **Recovery Strategy:** Listen to citizens' concerns empathetically. Establish forums for open dialogue, inviting citizens, experts, and opposition representatives to discuss issues and find common solutions.

Lessons Learned:

1. **Respect Freedom of the Press:** Freedom of the press is essential for a healthy democracy. Governments should allow journalists to report without fear of reprisal, even in times of crisis.

2. **Transparency Builds Trust:** Transparency and honesty are paramount. Providing accurate and timely information fosters trust among the public and international community.

3. **Engage Constructively:** Engage with citizens, journalists, and international stakeholders constructively. Listening and addressing concerns demonstrate a willingness to collaborate and find solutions.

4. **Avoid Suppressive Measures:** Suppressing dissent and criticism only exacerbate the crisis. Embrace diverse opinions and engage in open dialogue to find common ground.

By recognizing these errors and embracing a more transparent, empathetic, and inclusive approach, governments can navigate political crises more effectively, restoring public trust and fostering a sense of unity within the nation.

Case Study 4: Failed Media Relations Attempt in Economic Crisis

Background:

During a severe economic downturn, Company Y, a major corporation, faced a crisis due to financial mismanagement and ethical concerns. The company's media relations strategy failed to address the gravity of the situation, leading to investor panic, employee dissatisfaction, and a tarnished corporate image.

Identifying Errors:

1. **Misleading Financial Reporting:**

- **Error:** Company Y published misleading financial reports, projecting a positive outlook while concealing losses and debts. When the truth surfaced, it led to a loss of investor trust and credibility.

- **Recovery Strategy:** Adopt complete transparency in financial reporting. Provide accurate and realistic assessments, acknowledging challenges while outlining actionable plans for recovery.

2. **Lack of Accountability:**

- **Error:** Company Y's leadership failed to take accountability for the financial crisis, deflecting blame onto external factors. This lack of responsibility eroded trust among stakeholders.

- **Recovery Strategy:** Demonstrate leadership accountability. Accept responsibility for the situation, outline concrete steps for improvement, and hold individuals accountable for their actions or negligence.

3. **Inadequate Communication with Employees:**

- **Error:** Employees were left uninformed about the company's financial health, leading to rumors and anxiety. The lack of internal communication resulted in a demotivated workforce.

- **Recovery Strategy:** Prioritize internal communication. Keep employees informed about the company's situation, future plans, and measures being taken to address challenges. Engage in open dialogue to address concerns and boost employee morale.

4. **Ignoring Social Media Backlash:**

   - **Error:** Negative sentiments and criticisms on social media were ignored by Company Y, allowing the online narrative to spiral out of control.

   - **Recovery Strategy:** Actively monitor social media channels. Address concerns and criticisms promptly and professionally. Engage with customers and stakeholders, demonstrating a commitment to resolving issues and rebuilding trust.

Lessons Learned:

1. **Transparency and Honesty:** Open and honest communication, especially during a crisis, is indispensable. Misleading stakeholders or the public can lead to irreparable damage.

2. **Leadership Accountability:** Leaders must take responsibility for the crisis. Owning up to mistakes and outlining a clear path forward can restore confidence in leadership.

3. **Internal Communication:** Internal stakeholders, especially employees, must be kept well-informed. They are crucial ambassadors for the company's image and need to understand the company's situation.

4. **Social Media Engagement:** Social media is a powerful tool for communication. Ignoring online sentiment can amplify negative perceptions. Engaging proactively can help shape the narrative.

By acknowledging these errors and implementing a transparent, accountable, and communicative approach, companies facing economic crises can regain trust, stabilize their reputation, and pave the way for recovery and growth.

Case Study 5: Failed Media Relations Attempt in Human Rights Crisis

Background:

Country Z faced severe international scrutiny and condemnation due to human rights violations. The government's handling of the crisis through media relations exacerbated the situation, leading to diplomatic isolation, international sanctions, and a tarnished global reputation.

Identifying Errors:

1. **Denial and Deflection:**

- **Error:** The government denied allegations of human rights violations, dismissing international reports and deflecting blame onto opposition groups and external influences.

- **Recovery Strategy:** Acknowledge the allegations and conduct transparent investigations. Address human rights concerns openly and honestly, demonstrating a commitment to rectifying the situation.

2. **Lack of Cooperation with International Bodies:**

   - **Error:** Country Z refused cooperation with international human rights organizations and denied access for independent investigations, fueling suspicions and intensifying global criticism.

   - **Recovery Strategy:** Cooperate with reputable international human rights organizations. Allow independent investigations to validate the situation and showcase a willingness to work towards human rights improvements.

3. **Suppression of Dissent:**

   - **Error:** The government suppressed dissenting voices, including journalists, activists, and opposition figures, leading to a further erosion of trust and credibility.

- **Recovery Strategy:** Respect freedom of speech and freedom of assembly. Engage in open dialogue with dissenting voices, addressing their concerns and working towards inclusive policies.

4. **Failure to Address Vulnerable Populations:**

   - **Error:** Vulnerable populations affected by human rights violations were neglected in official communications, leaving their plight unheard and unaddressed.

   - **Recovery Strategy:** Prioritize the protection and support of vulnerable populations. Develop policies and programs specifically tailored to their needs. Ensure their voices are heard and respected in the national discourse.

Lessons Learned:

1. **Transparency and Accountability:** Transparency in addressing human rights issues and holding accountable those responsible are vital steps toward rebuilding credibility.

2. **International Cooperation:** Cooperation with international human rights bodies demonstrates a commitment to addressing concerns and finding solutions on a global scale.

3. **Respect for Freedom of Speech:** Respect for freedom of speech and dissenting voices fosters an atmosphere

of openness and dialogue, allowing for constructive discussions and resolutions.

4. **Inclusivity and Empathy:** Vulnerable populations must be prioritized. Their unique challenges and perspectives need to be acknowledged and integrated into policies and communication efforts.

By recognizing these errors and embracing a more transparent, inclusive, and cooperative approach, governments can navigate human rights crises more effectively, mitigating international criticism and working towards meaningful improvements in human rights practices.

Case Study 6: Recovering from a Controversial Municipal Project:

Background:

The municipal government of City A embarked on a controversial project to construct a large auto road through a cherished city park, aiming to alleviate traffic congestion. However, this decision sparked immense public outcry as citizens passionately protested the potential destruction of the park. The municipality's media relations strategy backfired, causing the public to lose trust in the government. The challenge was to recover from this failure and rebuild public confidence.

Identifying Errors:

1. **Lack of Public Consultation:**

- **Error:** The municipality failed to involve the public in the decision-making process, leading to resentment among citizens who felt their voices were not heard.

- **Recovery Strategy:** Organize town hall meetings, open forums, and online surveys to actively engage citizens. Listen to their concerns, demonstrating a commitment to inclusivity and democratic decision-making.

2. **Misallocation of Funds:**

- **Error:** Excessive spending on the road project and promotional campaigns that touted its benefits created public outrage when citizens disagreed with the project.

- **Recovery Strategy:** Reallocate funds to community initiatives and public services that directly benefit citizens. Be transparent about the reallocation, emphasizing the municipality's commitment to addressing community needs.

3. **Communication Breakdown:**

- **Error:** The municipality's communication was one-sided, promoting the project without addressing citizens' fears and concerns.

- **Recovery Strategy:** Initiate transparent and empathetic communication. Acknowledge public concerns, provide detailed project information, and explain how citizen input will be valued in future decisions.

4. **Failure to Highlight Alternatives:**

- **Error:** The municipality failed to explore and communicate alternative solutions to the traffic problem, making the road project appear as the only option.

- **Recovery Strategy:** Conduct an in-depth study of alternative traffic solutions, including public transportation improvements and traffic management strategies. Present these options to the public, inviting feedback and participation in the decision-making process.

Recovery Measures:

1. **Genuine Apology and Accountability:**

- The municipality should issue a sincere public apology for the lack of consultation and the misallocation of funds. Acknowledge the mistakes made and take accountability for the communication breakdown.

2. **Community Engagement and Listening Sessions:**

- Organize listening sessions where municipal officials actively listen to citizens' concerns and suggestions. Demonstrate a genuine willingness to incorporate public input into future projects.

3. **Project Redesign and Alternatives Assessment:**

- Reevaluate the road project, considering alternative routes that avoid the park. Involve urban planners, environmental experts, and citizen representatives in the redesign process to ensure a balanced solution.

4. **Transparency and Regular Updates:**

- Provide regular updates on the project's progress, challenges faced, and decisions made. Transparency fosters trust, showing the municipality's commitment to honest communication.

5. **Invest in Park Restoration and Community Initiatives:**

- Allocate funds to restore and enhance the park, ensuring it remains a cherished green space for the community. Invest in community initiatives, such as cultural events and recreational programs, to strengthen the municipality's relationship with citizens.

6. **Long-Term Citizen Engagement Strategy:**

- Develop a long-term citizen engagement strategy that involves citizens in municipal decision-making processes. Establish committees or councils representing diverse community interests to foster ongoing dialogue.

Rebuilding public trust requires genuine effort, empathy, and a commitment to inclusive governance. By actively involving citizens, addressing concerns, and making decisions collaboratively, the municipality can recover from this failure, demonstrating responsiveness to citizen needs and aspirations.

Expert Insights:

Elevating Media Relations Strategies with Professional Perspectives

In the realm of media relations, drawing upon the experiences and wisdom of seasoned professionals is akin to navigating uncharted waters with a trusty compass. Expert insights, obtained through in-depth interviews with media professionals, provide invaluable guidance, shaping successful media relations campaigns and fostering enduring relationships between organizations and the media landscape.

Delving into Expert Insights:

1. **Access to Specialized Knowledge:**

    - Media professionals, with their years of experience in journalism, public relations, and communication, possess specialized knowledge about the industry. These insights can range from understanding evolving media trends to comprehending the nuances of different journalistic styles and preferences.

- *Example:* Interviewing a senior editor from a leading news outlet allows your organization to gain insights into how journalists sift through press releases and select stories, enabling you to tailor your pitches effectively.

2. **Real-World Case Studies:**

- Media experts often bring real-world case studies to the table, detailing successful media relations campaigns and, crucially, the strategies that made them succeed. These case studies offer actionable takeaways, illustrating the dos and don'ts of media engagement.

- *Example:* An interview with a PR executive who orchestrated a viral social media campaign can provide valuable insights into crafting compelling narratives and leveraging social platforms for maximum impact.

3. **Effective Storytelling Techniques:**

- Experts can shed light on the art of storytelling, emphasizing the elements that captivate journalists and readers alike. Understanding how to structure a narrative, evoke emotions, and highlight the human aspect of a story is key to garnering media attention.

- *Example:* A conversation with a renowned journalist might reveal how personal anecdotes and relatable experiences enhance the appeal of a news story, influencing how your organization crafts its media narratives.

4. **Navigating Crisis Communication:**

- Media professionals have often been at the forefront of crisis situations, managing communication under intense pressure. Their insights can provide invaluable guidance on navigating crises, addressing public concerns, and mitigating reputational damage.

- *Example:* Speaking with a crisis communication expert who handled a high-profile corporate crisis can offer insights into managing media inquiries, addressing public skepticism, and rebuilding trust in the aftermath of a crisis.

Utilizing Expert Insights:

1. **Tailored Media Pitches:**

- Armed with expert insights, organizations can tailor their media pitches to align with journalists' preferences and industry standards. This personalized approach significantly increases the likelihood of journalists engaging with the pitched stories.

2. **Proactive Crisis Preparedness:**

- Expert insights on crisis communication can inform organizations' crisis preparedness plans.

Understanding potential challenges and effective response strategies equips organizations to handle crises with composure and agility.

3. **Enhanced Relationship Building:**

- By integrating expert perspectives into media relations strategies, organizations can build stronger, more authentic relationships with journalists. Acknowledging and respecting the media's expertise fosters a sense of partnership, leading to more fruitful collaborations.

4. **Continuous Learning and Adaptation:**

- Expert insights serve as a wellspring of knowledge for organizations, encouraging a culture of continuous learning and adaptation. Staying attuned to the evolving media landscape ensures that media relations strategies remain relevant and effective.

Incorporating expert insights into media relations efforts transforms campaigns from mere communications into powerful narratives that resonate with journalists and audiences alike. By embracing the wisdom shared by industry experts, organizations can navigate the complex media landscape with finesse, crafting compelling stories and establishing enduring connections with the media community.

Chapter 6: Future Trends in Media Relations

Impact of Technology on Media Relations:

The landscape of media relations is continually evolving, largely driven by technological advancements. In this digital age, staying ahead of the curve is imperative for successful communication strategies. Understanding the impact of technology is pivotal for organizations aiming to navigate the future of media relations.

Delving into Technological Impact:

1. **Instant Information Dissemination:**

   - Technology enables instantaneous dissemination of information across various platforms. Social media, news websites, and digital channels allow organizations to reach global audiences within seconds, revolutionizing the speed at which news travels.

   - *Example:* During a product launch, a well-crafted tweet or Instagram post can generate immediate buzz, reaching thousands of potential customers worldwide.

2. **Multimedia Storytelling:**

   - Advanced technology facilitates multimedia storytelling. Organizations can now combine text, images, videos, and interactive elements to create immersive narratives. This multimedia approach enhances engagement and ensures that messages resonate with diverse audiences.

- *Example:* Interactive infographics and virtual tours enable audiences to explore a brand's story visually, making the communication experience more captivating and memorable.

3. **Global Reach, Local Relevance:**

- Technology bridges geographical gaps, allowing organizations to engage with both global and local audiences. Tailoring messages to specific regions and cultures while maintaining a global brand identity is now achievable, ensuring messages are not lost in translation.

- *Example:* A multinational corporation can use geotargeting on social media to deliver region-specific content, acknowledging local events and holidays, thus enhancing relatability.

4. **Data-Driven Decision Making:**

- Technology provides robust data analytics tools that offer deep insights into audience behavior and preferences. Analyzing this data empowers organizations to refine their media strategies, ensuring they resonate with their target demographics effectively.

- *Example:* Utilizing data analytics, an e-commerce company can identify peak shopping times, allowing them to schedule press releases or promotions when the audience is most active and receptive.

5. **Real-time Engagement:**

  - Live streaming, interactive webinars, and social media live sessions enable real-time engagement with audiences. These platforms facilitate direct interaction, allowing organizations to address questions, concerns, and feedback instantaneously.

  - *Example:* A tech company can host a live Q&A session on social media, where product developers directly interact with customers, fostering a sense of community and building trust.

Understanding and harnessing the impact of technology enables organizations to create dynamic and impactful media relations strategies. Embracing these advancements ensures that communication efforts remain relevant, engaging, and influential in an increasingly digital world.

Artificial Intelligence and Data Analytics in Media Relations:

Artificial Intelligence (AI) and Data Analytics are revolutionizing the field of media relations, offering unprecedented insights and efficiency. By harnessing the power of AI and analytics, organizations can optimize their communication strategies, enhance audience engagement, and predict media trends with remarkable accuracy.

Delving into AI and Data Analytics:

1. **Automated Media Monitoring:**

   - AI-driven tools can monitor vast amounts of media data in real-time. These tools can track brand mentions, sentiment analysis, and even competitor activities. Automated monitoring ensures organizations stay updated on their media presence.

   - *Example:* An AI tool detects a sudden surge in negative sentiment online. Media relations professionals can swiftly respond, addressing concerns and mitigating reputational damage.

2. **Predictive Analytics:**

   - AI algorithms analyze historical data to predict future media trends. Predictive analytics enable organizations to anticipate topics that might capture media attention, allowing proactive preparation and strategic positioning.

- *Example:* By analyzing past media coverage patterns, AI predicts upcoming trends. A fashion brand can prepare press releases aligning with these trends, ensuring timely and relevant media coverage.

3. **Audience Segmentation:**

- AI algorithms analyze user behavior to create precise audience segments. Media relations strategies can then be tailored to address the specific interests and preferences of each segment, ensuring highly targeted and impactful communication.

- *Example:* An entertainment company identifies two distinct audience segments – young adults interested in comedy and families interested in animated movies. Tailored press releases and media events are crafted for each segment, maximizing engagement.

4. **Chatbots and Virtual Assistants:**

- AI-powered chatbots and virtual assistants enhance media interactions. These tools can handle routine inquiries, provide information, and even schedule media appointments, freeing up human resources for more strategic tasks.

- *Example:* A media outlet's chatbot provides journalists with event schedules, press materials, and interview opportunities, streamlining the information dissemination process.

5. **Content Optimization:**

   - AI tools analyze content performance metrics to optimize press releases, articles, and multimedia materials. Insights on what type of content resonates most with the audience enable organizations to refine their messaging for maximum impact.

   - *Example:* By analyzing which headlines and visuals receive the most engagement, AI suggests the optimal combination for future press releases, ensuring they capture media attention effectively.

The integration of AI and data analytics in media relations empowers organizations to make informed decisions, enhance audience engagement, and strategically position their messages in the evolving media landscape. Embracing these technologies is pivotal for staying ahead in a competitive and dynamic media environment.

Virtual Reality and Augmented Reality in Media Outreach:

Virtual Reality (VR) and Augmented Reality (AR) have transcended the realm of entertainment, finding profound applications in media relations. These immersive technologies offer unique opportunities for organizations to captivate audiences, tell compelling stories, and create memorable media experiences.

Delving into VR and AR in Media Outreach:

1. **Immersive Storytelling:**

   - VR and AR enable immersive storytelling experiences. Organizations can create virtual tours, 360-degree videos, and interactive AR elements within physical spaces. These immersive narratives allow journalists and audiences to engage with the story on a deeper level.

   - *Example:* A tourism board creates a VR experience showcasing popular destinations. Journalists can virtually explore these locations, providing them with firsthand insights for their travel features.

2. **Product Demonstrations:**

   - VR and AR facilitate virtual product demonstrations. Companies can showcase their products in a virtual environment, allowing journalists to interact with the products as if they were physically present. This hands-on experience enhances product understanding and coverage quality.

- *Example:* An automobile manufacturer develops an AR app that allows journalists to visualize and interact with the latest car models. Journalists can explore the interior, customize features, and even take virtual test drives.

3. **Event Coverage and Virtual Press Conferences:**

- VR technology enables remote event attendance. Journalists can participate in events, product launches, and press conferences virtually, providing a seamless experience. AR overlays can enhance live event coverage, offering real-time information and context.

- *Example:* A tech company hosts a product launch event in VR. Journalists from around the world attend the event virtually, interacting with company representatives, exploring product demos, and asking questions in real-time.

4. **Interactive Media Releases:**

- VR and AR can transform traditional press releases into interactive experiences. Companies can embed AR elements in physical press materials, allowing journalists to scan printed materials with their smartphones to reveal additional multimedia content, such as videos, animations, and infographics.

- *Example:* A publishing house releases a physical book with AR-enhanced pages. Journalists can scan specific pages with an AR app, revealing author interviews, behind-the-scenes videos, and interactive character profiles.

5. **Virtual Reality Interviews and Documentaries:**

- VR interviews and documentaries offer immersive experiences for journalists and audiences. Organizations can conduct virtual interviews with key personnel or create VR documentaries that provide in-depth insights into their operations, projects, or social initiatives.

- *Example:* An environmental organization creates a VR documentary highlighting their conservation efforts. Journalists don VR headsets and virtually accompany researchers into the field, witnessing their work firsthand.

By leveraging VR and AR technologies in media outreach, organizations can create unforgettable experiences that resonate with journalists and audiences. These immersive strategies not only enhance media coverage but also position organizations as innovators in their industries, capturing the attention of media professionals and the public alike.

Deep Dive into Future Trends in Media Relations:

Navigating the Uncharted Territory

As the media landscape continues its rapid evolution, media relations professionals are confronted with a diverse array of challenges and opportunities. In this chapter, we embark on a profound exploration of the future trends in media relations, delving into the intricate world of AI-driven media outreach and immersive technologies. By comprehensively understanding these emerging trends, organizations can effectively navigate the complexities of the digital age, leveraging innovative strategies to capture attention and engage audiences.

Delving into Future Trends:

1. **AI-Driven Media Outreach:**

    - *Challenges:* With the integration of AI in media outreach, the challenge lies in striking the delicate balance between automation and authenticity. Ensuring that AI-generated content maintains the human touch, empathy, and relevance is crucial to prevent alienating audiences.

    - *Opportunities:* AI offers unparalleled opportunities for hyper-personalization. By analyzing vast datasets, AI tools can craft tailored messages, predict media trends, and even anticipate journalists' preferences. This precision targeting ensures that pitches resonate with recipients, enhancing the likelihood of media coverage.

- *Example:* A fashion brand utilizes AI algorithms to analyze fashion editors' past articles and social media interactions. AI generates pitches tailored to each editor's style, increasing the chances of securing features in prominent fashion magazines.

2. **Immersive Technologies:**

- *Challenges:* Immersive technologies like VR and AR demand significant investment in hardware and software development. Ensuring accessibility and affordability for journalists and audiences is a challenge, especially for smaller organizations with limited resources.

- *Opportunities:* Immersive technologies offer unparalleled storytelling experiences. VR enables journalists to transport audiences to distant locations, while AR overlays contextual information in real-time. These immersive narratives create deep emotional connections, leaving a lasting impact on audiences.

- *Example:* A travel agency employs VR to create virtual tours of exotic destinations. Journalists and potential travelers can don VR headsets and explore resorts, beaches, and cultural landmarks, fostering a strong desire to experience these destinations firsthand.

3. **Ethical Considerations and Data Privacy:**

   - *Challenges:* The use of AI and immersive technologies raises ethical concerns regarding data privacy, consent, and the potential misuse of personal information. Striking a balance between innovation and ethical practices is essential to maintain public trust.

   - *Opportunities:* Organizations can lead by example, adopting transparent data practices and stringent privacy protocols. By prioritizing user consent and data security, organizations can build trust with both journalists and audiences, ensuring ethical media relations practices.

   - *Example:* A tech company developing AR applications explicitly outlines how user data will be utilized. Users must provide explicit consent before accessing AR features, demonstrating the company's commitment to ethical data usage.

4. **Collaborative Journalism and Crowdsourced Content:**

   - *Challenges:* Collaborative journalism and crowdsourced content rely on user participation.

Encouraging active engagement and managing diverse contributions while maintaining journalistic standards pose challenges in ensuring content quality and accuracy.

- *Opportunities:* Collaborative journalism fosters community engagement and inclusivity. By allowing diverse voices to contribute to media narratives, organizations can create authentic, community-driven stories that resonate deeply with audiences.

- *Example:* A news organization invites citizens to share their perspectives on local issues through an online platform. User-generated content, including videos, photos, and testimonials, enriches news stories, providing a holistic view of community experiences.

Strategic Considerations:

1. **Education and Training:**

   - Organizations must invest in training their media relations teams to harness the full potential of AI tools and immersive technologies. Educating professionals about ethical considerations and best practices is essential to uphold industry standards.

2. **Agile Adaptation:**

   - Media relations strategies should remain agile, adapting to emerging technologies and trends swiftly. Proactive experimentation with new tools ensures organizations stay ahead of the curve, embracing innovations that enhance communication efforts.

3. **Ethical Frameworks:**

   - Developing clear ethical frameworks and guidelines for the use of AI and immersive technologies is paramount. Organizations must prioritize user consent, data privacy, and content accuracy, aligning their practices with ethical standards to maintain credibility.

4. **Community Engagement:**

   - Fostering community engagement through collaborative journalism enhances trust and loyalty. Organizations should actively seek input from their communities, valuing diverse perspectives and incorporating them into media narratives.

In this era of rapid technological advancement, embracing the future trends in media relations demands a strategic blend of innovation, ethical considerations, and community-centric approaches. By navigating the challenges and harnessing the opportunities presented by AI-driven media outreach and immersive technologies, organizations can revolutionize their media relations strategies, ensuring they remain compelling, relevant, and impactful in the ever-changing digital landscape.

Chapter 7: Additional Sections

Interactive Elements: Enhancing Media Relations Mastery

Building upon the foundation laid in previous chapters, this section further immerses readers in the intricacies of media relations. By providing an array of interactive elements, exercises, and templates, this chapter empowers readers to refine their skills, apply theoretical knowledge, and hone their expertise in the dynamic field of media relations.

Delving into Interactive Elements:

1. **Media Pitch Workshops:**

    - *Description:* Engage readers in simulated media pitch workshops. Provide fictional scenarios where readers craft pitches tailored to different media outlets and journalist profiles. Encourage creative thinking and strategic messaging to garner media interest.

    - *Objective:* Enhance readers' ability to customize pitches effectively, considering various media preferences and audience expectations. Provide feedback on pitch quality, emphasizing the importance of relevance and clarity.

    - *Example:* Readers are tasked with pitching a groundbreaking scientific discovery to both mainstream news outlets and specialized science magazines. They must adapt their language and approach to suit the interests of each media segment.

2. **Case Study Analysis:**

- *Description:* Present detailed case studies of successful media relations campaigns. Encourage readers to analyze these cases, identifying key strategies, challenges faced, and the impact achieved. Discuss the outcomes, enabling readers to glean insights from real-world examples.

- *Objective:* Develop readers' analytical skills, allowing them to dissect media relations campaigns critically. By understanding the nuances of successful strategies, readers can implement similar approaches in their own initiatives.

- *Example:* Analyze a case study where a startup gained widespread media coverage. Discuss the timing of their press releases, the engagement strategies employed, and the role of influencers. Readers identify actionable takeaways for their own campaigns.

3. **Media Outreach Templates:**

- *Description:* Provide readers with customizable templates for various media outreach materials, including press releases, media alerts, and journalist introduction emails. Explain the essential components of each template and offer tips on tailoring them for specific purposes.

- *Objective:* Equip readers with practical tools to streamline their media outreach efforts. By using professionally crafted templates as a starting point, readers can focus on adapting the content to suit their unique stories and target audiences.

- *Example:* Offer a press release template for product launches. Highlight the importance of a compelling headline, concise product description, and engaging call-to-action. Readers personalize the template for their own product launches, ensuring impactful media coverage.

4. **Interactive Quizzes and Assessments:**

   - *Description:* Develop interactive quizzes that assess readers' knowledge of media relations concepts, best practices, and case studies. Include multiple-choice questions, scenario-based challenges, and situational analyses. Provide instant feedback and explanations for correct and incorrect answers.

   - *Objective:* Reinforce readers' understanding of key media relations concepts through engaging assessments. Interactive quizzes encourage active learning, allowing readers to identify areas for improvement and reinforcing their grasp of essential topics.

- *Example:* Pose a scenario where a company faces a sudden PR crisis. Ask readers to choose the most appropriate initial response from a list of options. Explain the consequences of each choice, helping readers comprehend crisis management strategies.

5. **Expert Interviews and Insights:**

- *Description:* Continue the series of expert interviews, featuring media professionals, PR strategists, and journalists. Explore diverse topics, including emerging media trends, crisis communication, and the future of journalism. Encourage readers to submit questions for upcoming interviews.

- *Objective:* Provide readers with access to industry expertise and diverse perspectives. Expert interviews offer valuable insights, enabling readers to stay informed about the latest developments in media relations and adapt their strategies accordingly.

- *Example:* Conduct an interview with a renowned investigative journalist. Discuss the role of investigative reporting in shaping public opinion and strategies for organizations to engage with investigative journalists ethically.

By incorporating these interactive elements into the handbook, readers are not merely passive recipients of information but active participants in their learning journey. Through practical exercises, real-world case analyses, customizable templates, interactive quizzes, and expert insights, readers are equipped with a comprehensive toolkit to excel in the dynamic realm of media relations. This immersive approach ensures that readers not only grasp theoretical concepts but also develop practical skills, preparing them to navigate the complexities of media relations with confidence and expertise.

Glossary of Terms:

Decoding the Language of Media Relations
In the intricate world of media relations, a nuanced understanding of terminology is indispensable. This comprehensive glossary serves as a reliable companion, providing readers with clear and concise definitions of key media relations terms. By decoding the language of media relations, readers can enhance their comprehension, communicate effectively, and navigate the field with confidence.

Delving into the Glossary:

1. **Media Relations:**

    - *Definition:* Media relations refers to the strategic communication efforts of organizations to establish and maintain relationships with journalists, influencers, and media outlets. The goal is to secure favorable media coverage, manage public perception, and disseminate key messages to target audiences.

2. **Press Release:**

   - *Definition:* A press release is an official statement issued by an organization to the media. It provides newsworthy information about the organization, such as product launches, events, achievements, or announcements. Press releases aim to attract media attention and secure media coverage.

3. **Pitch:**

   - *Definition:* A pitch is a concise and persuasive message presented to journalists or media outlets to persuade them to cover a particular story or topic. Pitches are tailored to the interests of the recipients and highlight the relevance and significance of the story for their audience.

4. **Media Kit:**

   - *Definition:* A media kit, also known as a press kit, is a collection of promotional materials and information about an organization or event. It typically includes press releases, high-resolution images, bios, and relevant background information. Media kits are designed to assist journalists in their coverage.

5. **Crisis Communication:**

- *Definition:* Crisis communication refers to the strategic communication efforts employed by organizations during emergencies, crises, or challenging situations. The goal is to manage the organization's reputation, address public concerns, and provide accurate information to stakeholders and the media.

6. **Background Briefing:**

- *Definition:* A background briefing is an off-the-record meeting between organization representatives and journalists. During such briefings, organizations provide additional context, background information, and insights about a specific issue or event. Journalists attend background briefings to deepen their understanding before reporting.

7. **Embargo:**

- *Definition:* An embargo is an arrangement between an organization and a journalist, specifying a date and time when certain information, such as a press release, can be publicly released or reported. Journalists agree not to publish the information before the embargoed time.

8. **Media Monitoring:**

   - *Definition:* Media monitoring involves tracking and analyzing media coverage related to an organization, individual, or specific topics. Media monitoring tools gather information from various media sources, allowing organizations to assess their media presence, track sentiment, and respond to coverage effectively.

9. **Influencer Marketing:**

   - *Definition:* Influencer marketing is a marketing strategy that involves collaborating with influencers, individuals with significant online followings, to promote products, services, or brands. Influencers create authentic content, reaching a wide audience and influencing their purchasing decisions.

10. **Media Outlet:**

   - *Definition:* A media outlet refers to a specific platform or channel used to disseminate news and information. Media outlets can include newspapers, magazines, television stations, radio stations, online news portals, blogs, and social media platforms.

This glossary serves as an invaluable resource, providing readers with the foundation to comprehend media relations terminology effectively. By mastering these definitions, readers can engage in meaningful conversations, craft precise messages, and navigate the complexities of media relations with precision and expertise.

Frequently Asked Questions (FAQs):

Navigating Media Relations Queries

In the dynamic realm of media relations, questions often arise, reflecting the complexities and nuances of engaging with the media effectively. This section aims to provide clarity and guidance by addressing common queries and concerns related to media relations. By delving into these frequently asked questions, readers can deepen their understanding, resolve uncertainties, and approach media interactions with confidence and expertise.

Delving into Frequently Asked Questions (FAQs):

1. **Q1: What Is the Role of Media Relations in an Organization?**

   - **A:** Media relations plays a pivotal role in managing an organization's reputation and public image. It involves establishing and nurturing relationships with journalists, influencers, and media outlets to secure positive media coverage, disseminate key messages, and respond to public inquiries effectively.

2. **Q2: How Can I Build Effective Relationships with Journalists?**

   - **A:** Building effective relationships with journalists requires personalized outreach, understanding their interests, and respecting their preferences for communication. Face-to-face meetings, attending industry events, and providing timely and relevant information are key strategies for nurturing these relationships.

3. **Q3: What Constitutes a Newsworthy Story for the Media?**

   - **A:** A newsworthy story is one that is timely, relevant, and interesting to the target audience of the media outlet. Events such as product launches, significant achievements, innovative initiatives, and community engagement often capture media attention. Uniqueness, impact, and human interest elements also enhance a story's newsworthiness.

4. **Q4: How Do I Craft an Engaging Press Release?**

   - **A:** An engaging press release is concise, clear, and focused on the most important information. Start with a compelling headline, followed by a concise summary of the news. Include relevant quotes, high-quality visuals, and contact information for media inquiries. Tailor the

136

content to the interests of the target media outlets.

5. **Q5: What Should I Do During a PR Crisis?**

- **A:** During a PR crisis, transparency, honesty, and swift communication are paramount. Acknowledge the issue, provide accurate information, and outline the steps being taken to address the situation. Designate a spokesperson, monitor media coverage, and respond promptly to inquiries. Additionally, prepare a crisis communication plan in advance to guide your response.

6. **Q6: How Can I Leverage Social Media in Media Relations?**

- **A:** Social media platforms offer avenues for direct engagement with the media and the public. Regularly share relevant content, engage with journalists and influencers, and participate in industry conversations. Social media also allows for real-time updates during events and announcements, amplifying media coverage.

7. **Q7: What Is the Significance of Media Monitoring?**

- **A:** Media monitoring involves tracking and analyzing media coverage to assess an organization's media presence and public sentiment. It helps in understanding the impact of media relations efforts, identifying emerging trends, and making informed decisions. Media monitoring tools provide valuable insights for strategic planning and response.

8. **Q8: How Can I Measure the Success of a Media Relations Campaign?**

   - **A:** The success of a media relations campaign can be measured through various metrics, including media mentions, reach, sentiment analysis, website traffic generated from media coverage, and audience engagement on social media. Analyze these metrics to evaluate the campaign's impact and adjust strategies for future initiatives.

By addressing these frequently asked questions, readers gain practical insights and actionable strategies to navigate the complexities of media relations successfully. Armed with knowledge and understanding, media relations professionals can proactively approach challenges, seize opportunities, and build enduring relationships with the media, fostering positive and impactful interactions.

Chapter 8: Conclusion

Summary of Key Takeaways

In the ever-evolving landscape of media relations, this handbook has journeyed through the essential principles, strategies, and nuances that define successful engagements with the media. As we conclude this comprehensive guide, it is essential to reflect on the key takeaways and reinforce the foundational principles that underpin effective media relations.

1. **Embracing Relationships:** Media relations is fundamentally about relationships – cultivating trust, understanding, and mutual respect with journalists, influencers, and media outlets. These relationships form the bedrock upon which successful media coverage is built.

2. **Adaptability and Innovation:** The media landscape is continuously shifting, driven by technological advancements and changing audience behaviors. Media relations professionals must remain agile, embracing innovative technologies, strategies, and storytelling methods to capture and retain audience attention.

3. **Transparency and Authenticity:** Honest and transparent communication is the cornerstone of

effective media relations. Organizations must uphold ethical standards, ensuring that their messages are authentic, accurate, and aligned with their actions. Transparency fosters credibility and credibility strengthens media relationships.

4. **Strategic Planning:** Media relations cannot thrive without meticulous planning. From identifying newsworthy stories to crafting compelling pitches, every step must be guided by a well-thought-out strategy. Research, analysis, and proactive planning are essential elements of successful media engagement.

5. **Continuous Learning:** The world of media relations is dynamic, with new trends, tools, and challenges emerging regularly. Media relations professionals must be avid learners, staying informed about industry developments, evolving media platforms, and emerging technologies to stay ahead of the curve.

6. **Ethical Engagement:** Ethical conduct is non-negotiable in media relations. Upholding the highest standards of integrity in interactions with the media, respecting embargo agreements, safeguarding data privacy, and ensuring truthful communication are imperative for maintaining professional credibility.

Closing Thoughts:

As we conclude this handbook, it is our hope that the knowledge and insights shared within these pages empower you to navigate the complexities of media relations with confidence and proficiency. Remember that media relations is a dynamic dance of strategy, relationships, and adaptability. By embracing the principles outlined in this guide, you are well-equipped to not only face the challenges of the media landscape but also leverage its vast opportunities.

May your media relations endeavors be marked by meaningful connections, impactful storytelling, and enduring positive influence. Here's to building bridges, shaping narratives, and making a lasting impact in the world of media relations. Safe travels on your media relations journey, and may your stories find their rightful place in the hearts and minds of your audience.

Encouragement for Continuous Learning:

Nurturing Expertise in Media Relations

In the ever-evolving realm of media relations, the pursuit of knowledge is not just a choice; it is a necessity. Encouraging continuous learning is akin to nurturing a garden – it yields blossoms of expertise, innovation, and adaptability. Here's why fostering a culture of perpetual learning is essential in the world of media relations:

1. **Staying Ahead of Trends:** The media landscape is dynamic, shaped by emerging technologies, shifting audience preferences, and novel storytelling methods. Continuous learning ensures that media relations professionals remain abreast of these trends, enabling

them to harness new opportunities and navigate challenges effectively.

2. **Adapting to Technological Advancements:** Technology is the heartbeat of modern media. Embracing tools like AI-driven analytics, immersive virtual reality, and interactive social media platforms demands a deep understanding. Continuous learning equips professionals to leverage these technologies, enhancing the impact of media relations efforts.

3. **Enhancing Strategic Thinking:** Learning from case studies, industry analyses, and expert insights refines strategic thinking. Exposure to diverse perspectives sharpens the ability to craft targeted pitches, identify newsworthy angles, and design impactful media campaigns. Continuous learning is the crucible where raw knowledge transforms into strategic acumen.

4. **Fostering Ethical Practices:** Media ethics, including transparency, accuracy, and responsible reporting, are foundational. Continuous learning deepens ethical awareness, helping professionals navigate ethical dilemmas, maintain credibility, and uphold the integrity of media relations engagements.

5. **Cultivating Versatility:** Media relations professionals wear many hats – from storytellers and crisis managers to relationship builders and data analysts. Continuous learning hones these multifaceted skills, fostering versatility and enabling professionals to

adapt their roles to the evolving demands of the media landscape.

6. **Building a Network of Expertise:** Learning is not solitary; it thrives in communities of knowledge. Actively participating in industry forums, attending conferences, and engaging in collaborative learning endeavors create a network of expertise. This network becomes a wellspring of ideas, mentorship, and collaborative opportunities, enriching the learning journey.

Encouragement in Action:

- **Online Courses and Webinars:** Enroll in online courses and webinars focused on media relations, journalism ethics, and emerging technologies. Platforms like Coursera, edX, and industry-specific organizations offer diverse, expert-led courses.

- **Professional Workshops:** Attend workshops and seminars conducted by media experts and PR professionals. These immersive events provide hands-on experiences, allowing you to apply theoretical knowledge to real-world scenarios.

- **Industry Conferences:** Participate in industry conferences and summits where thought leaders converge. Engage in panel discussions, Q&A sessions, and networking events. These interactions expose you to diverse perspectives and foster meaningful connections.

- **Mentorship:** Seek mentorship from experienced media relations professionals. Learning from their experiences, challenges, and successes offers invaluable insights and guidance. Mentorship relationships often extend your learning beyond formal settings.

- **Reading and Research:** Cultivate a habit of reading industry publications, research papers, and case studies. Stay informed about the latest trends, best practices, and innovative campaigns. Engaging with thought-provoking literature broadens your understanding and nurtures critical thinking.

Remember, in the world of media relations, knowledge is not static; it is a river that flows ceaselessly. Embrace this ever-flowing stream, for within its currents lie the secrets to mastering the art and science of media relations. Stay curious, stay engaged, and keep learning. Your journey toward media relations excellence has only just begun.

Acknowledgments and Credits:

Gratitude in the Tapestry of Media Relations

As we reach the culmination of this handbook on media relations, it is essential to acknowledge the collective efforts, wisdom, and support that have woven this tapestry of knowledge. The creation of this comprehensive guide has been a collaborative endeavor, drawing inspiration and insights from a multitude of sources. In this spirit of gratitude, we extend our heartfelt acknowledgments:

1. **Expert Contributors:** We express our sincere gratitude to the media relations experts, seasoned journalists, and communication professionals whose knowledge and experiences have illuminated the pages of this handbook. Their invaluable insights have been the guiding stars of this journey.

2. **Case Study Participants:** Our heartfelt thanks to the organizations and individuals who generously shared their real-world experiences through case studies. These stories have not only enriched the content but also provided readers with tangible examples of successful media relations strategies in action.

3. **Industry Thought Leaders:** We extend our appreciation to the thought leaders and influencers in the field of media relations. Their pioneering work, innovative campaigns, and thought-provoking ideas have shaped the landscape of media relations, inspiring professionals worldwide.

4. **Educational Institutions:** We acknowledge the contributions of educational institutions, professors, and researchers who have dedicated their efforts to advancing the knowledge and understanding of media relations. Their research and teachings have provided the foundation upon which this handbook stands.

5. **Media Outlets:** Our thanks to the various media outlets, publications, and online platforms that disseminate knowledge, news, and insights. Your dedication to journalistic integrity and the pursuit of truth forms the bedrock of the media relations profession.

6. **Readers and Professionals:** To the readers and media relations professionals, your curiosity, engagement, and passion for learning have been the driving force behind this endeavor. Your feedback and enthusiasm have elevated the content, making it a shared creation.

7. **Supportive Communities:** We express our gratitude to the supportive communities within the media relations industry. The spirit of collaboration, knowledge sharing, and mentorship within these communities has fostered an environment where professionals can thrive and learn from one another.

8. **Supporting Organizations:** Our thanks to the organizations and institutions that support the continuous learning and professional development of media relations professionals. Your commitment to education and skill enhancement is instrumental in shaping the future of the industry.

Closing Thoughts:

In the vast and interconnected world of media relations, each thread of knowledge, every shared experience, and all expressions of gratitude contribute to the rich tapestry that defines our collective understanding. As we acknowledge the diverse contributors and supporters, we recognize that our journey in media relations is not solitary; it is a shared expedition, enriched by the wisdom and generosity of many.

With deep gratitude, we celebrate the collaborative spirit that has made this handbook possible. May the knowledge shared here continue to inspire, educate, and empower media relations professionals, fostering meaningful connections and impactful engagements in the ever-evolving media landscape. Thank you, one and all, for being part of this enriching odyssey.

Resources for Further Reading: Nurturing Knowledge Beyond the Horizon

Embarking on a journey in media relations is not just about mastering the fundamentals; it's a continuous exploration, a perpetual quest for knowledge that shapes expertise. In the realm of media relations, the thirst for understanding finds its quenching in the pages of books, research papers, industry journals, and insightful blogs. Here, we present a curated selection of resources for further reading, offering a diverse tapestry of perspectives and expertise.

1. **Books on Media Relations:**

- *"Media Relations: Issues and Strategies" by Jane Johnston*

- *"Effective Media Relations: How to Get Results" by Michael Bland*

- *"Media Relations in Property" by Peter Smith and Michael Bland*

- *"Media Relations Handbook for Agencies, Associations, Nonprofits, and Congress" by Bradford Fitch*

2. Industry Publications and Journals:

- *Public Relations Review* - A scholarly journal focusing on public relations theory and practice.

- *Journalism Studies* - An academic journal exploring journalism and journalistic communication in all its forms.

3. Online Resources and Blogs:

- *PR Daily* - An online publication offering news, advice, and opinions on public relations, marketing, and social media.

- *Spin Sucks* - A digital platform providing insights into communication, PR, and marketing strategies.

4. Professional Organizations:

- *Public Relations Society of America (PRSA)* - A professional organization offering resources, webinars, and publications on media relations best practices.

- *International Association of Business Communicators (IABC)* - A global network providing resources and professional development opportunities for communication professionals.

5. **Research Papers and Case Studies:**

- Explore academic databases like *Google Scholar* and *ResearchGate* for research papers on media relations, crisis communication, and journalism ethics. These platforms host a wealth of scholarly articles and case studies.

6. **Industry Conferences and Events:**

- Attend industry conferences such as the *International Public Relations Research Conference (IPRRC)* and the *Global Communication Association (GCA) Conference* to access cutting-edge research presentations and network with experts.

7. **Media Relations Blogs and Thought Leaders:**

- Follow media relations thought leaders and experts on platforms like *LinkedIn* and *Twitter*. Their blogs and posts often share insights, analyses, and best practices in real time.

8. **Online Courses and Webinars:**

- Enroll in online courses on platforms like *Coursera* and *Udemy* that cover media relations, crisis communication, and digital PR strategies. Webinars hosted by industry experts provide interactive learning experiences.

Conclusion:

As you delve into these resources, remember that the pursuit of knowledge is a dynamic and enriching endeavor. Each book, article, and conversation broadens your understanding, shaping you into a more adept and insightful media relations professional. The horizon of learning is infinite, and in this endless expanse, you'll find inspiration, innovation, and the seeds of transformative ideas.

May your reading endeavors be enlightening, your discoveries profound, and your expertise ever-expanding. With each turn of the page, you venture deeper into the vibrant tapestry of media relations, uncovering the wisdom that propels your journey toward mastery. Happy reading!

About Author

Osman Karakas is an accomplished journalist, editor, researcher, photographer, and author with a diverse and extensive background in the field of journalism. With a passion for storytelling and a commitment to journalistic integrity, Osman Karakas has made significant contributions to the media industry throughout his career.

Osman Karakas has been recognized for his outstanding work and has received numerous awards and accolades. In 1991, he was honored with the Excellence in Journalism award by the Deadline Club-Society of Professional Journalists in New York, USA.

In 1990, Osman Karakas won first place in the Spot News category at the Associated Press Association, New York, for his impactful news story titled "Don't Let Him Die" published in the New York Post.

He also received the prestigious Picture of the Year Award in 1990 from the University of Missouri - School of Journalism/National Press Photographers Association, his photography was compared to Michelangelo's "Pieta" by the head of the jury.

His international experience continued as they worked as a correspondent at the United Nations for Anadolu Weekly in New York, USA, and later as a Correspondent and News & Photo Editor for Hurriyet International Daily, covering press conferences at the UN.

In addition to his international assignments, Osman Karakas his career in journalism as a correspondent for TRT (Turkish Radio & Television) in Turkmenistan and Kazakhstan from 1993 to 1996. During this time, they also served as the Editor-in-Chief of the TURKCAN International Magazine in Turkmenistan. Also manager and editor-in-Chief various newspapers and magazines in Türkiye and Central Asia.

Osman Karakas has been involved in academia as well, having worked as a Lecturer at Manas University in Bishkek, Kyrgyzstan, where they taught journalism courses, advised students, and served on various committees about 8 years. His dedication to education and knowledge sharing has been instrumental in nurturing the next generation of journalists.

With proficiency in multiple languages, including English, Turkish, Russian, Turkmen, Azerbaijan, Kyrgyz, and Kazakh, Osman Karakas has been able to communicate and report on diverse topics with cultural sensitivity and understanding. his language skills have allowed them to engage with various communities and provide insightful coverage.

Alongside his journalistic career, Osman Karakas has authored several books and documentaries, covering topics ranging from journalism to detective novels and documentaries on historical events. They have also exhibited his photography in multiple personal exhibitions in Turkey and Kyrgyzstan, showcasing his artistic talent and unique perspective.

Osman Karakas possesses a wide range of skills and expertise, including diplomacy, media relations, public relations, political campaign management, managing media, photography, communication, and web publishing. Including; advertising, social media, and desktop publishing, keeping up with the evolving landscape of digital journalism.

In conclusion, Osman Karakas has made significant contributions to the field of journalism through his exceptional work, awards, publications, and dedication to journalistic ethics. His diverse experiences, international exposure, and commitment to storytelling have shaped his career and established them as a respected figure in the media industry.

Recommended Books

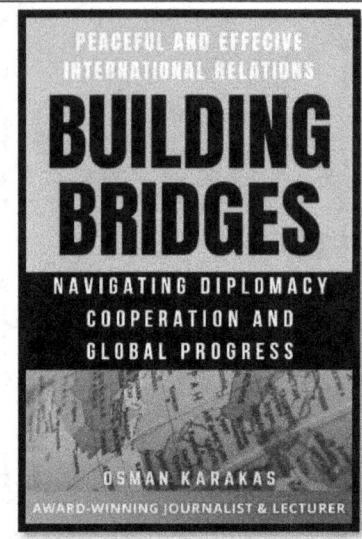

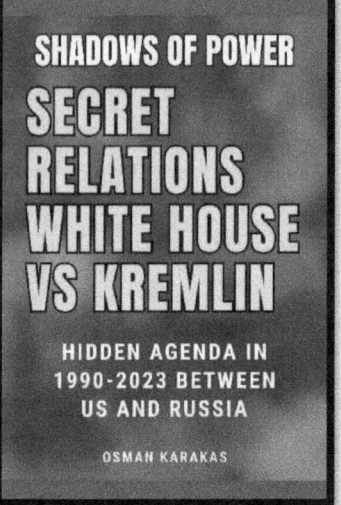

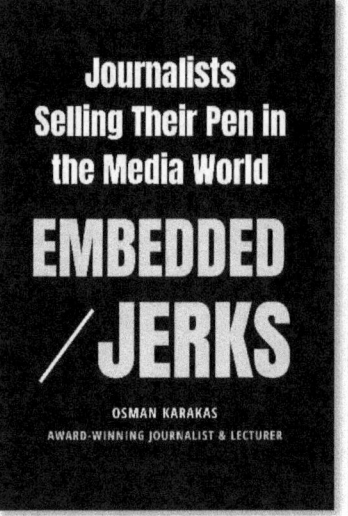

The collection of books is accessible for purchase on Amazon.com platform.